The Gift and the Promise

Becoming What We Are in Christ

Kaleidoscope

Statement of Purpose

Kaleidoscope is a series of adult educational resources developed for the ecumenical church by Lancaster Theological Seminary and the United Church Board for Homeland Ministries. Developed for adults who want serious study and dialogue on contemporary issues of Christian faith and life, Kaleidoscope offers elective resources designed to provide new knowledge and new understanding for persons who seek personal growth and a deeper sense of social responsibility in their lives.

Kaleidoscope utilizes the expertise of professionals in various disciplines to develop study resources in both print and video. The series also provides tools to help persons develop skills in studying, reflecting, inquiring critically, and exploring avenues of appropriate Christian responses in life.

Kaleidoscope provides sound and tested resources in theology, biblical studies, ethics, and other related subjects that link personal growth and social responsibility to life situations in which adult Christian persons develop.

The Gift and the Promise

Becoming What We Are in Christ

Peter Schmiechen

A Kaleidoscope Series Resource

United Church Press

New York

KALEIDOSCOPE SERIES

Library of Congress Cataloging-in-Publication Data

Schmiechen, Peter.
    The gift and the promise : becoming what we are in Christ /
Peter Schmiechen.

    (A Kaleidoscope series resource)
    Includes bibliographical references.
    ISBN 0-8298-0838-8
    1. Conversation. I. Title. II. Series.
BT780.S32   1990
248.2'4—dc20   89-49764
                                                CIP

United Church Press, 475 Riverside Drive, New York, N.Y. 10015

To
Jan
A Canterbury Pilgrim

How to Use the Kaleidoscope Series

The Kaleidoscope book is the basic resource for all students in the Kaleidoscope Series. For each Kaleidoscope book there is a Leader's Guide edition, which has a sixteen-page Leader's Guide bound into the back of the book. The leader will need to study both the text and the Leader's Guide to prepare to lead study sessions of the Kaleidoscope Series resources.

Contents

Introduction to the Kaleidoscope Series ix

Preface xi

1. Turning 1

2. The Gift 13

3. Expanding Our View of Faith 25

4. A Model of Conversion 38

5. Surveying the Contours and Boundaries of Our
   Hearts 52

6. Living in the Promise 67

Bibliography 85

Introduction to the Kaleidoscope Series

Through direct experience, our faculty at Lancaster Theological Seminary discovered that a continual demand exists for Christian theological reflection upon issues of current interest. To meet this demand, the Seminary for many years has offered courses for lay people. To offer the substance of these courses to the wider Christian public is the purpose of the Kaleidoscope Series.

Lancaster Seminary exists to proclaim the gospel of Jesus Christ for the sake of the church and the world. In addition to preparing men and women for the ordained Christian ministry, the Seminary seeks to be a center of theological reflection for clergy and laity. Continuing education and leadership development for all Christians focus our mission. The topics and educational style in the Kaleidoscope Series extend Lancaster Seminary's commitment: theological study reflective of the interaction of the Bible, the world, the church, worship, and personal faith. We hope that this course will provide an opportunity for you to grow in self-understanding, in knowledge of other people and God's creation, and in the spirit of Christ.

We wish to thank the staff of the Division of Education and Publication of the United Church Board for Homeland Ministries for their leadership in this enterprise. The Rev. Dr. Ansley Coe Throckmorton, The Rev. Dr. Larry E. Kalp, and The Rev. Dr. Percel O. Alston provided encouragement and support for the project. In particular, we are grateful for the inspiration of Percel Alston, who was a trustee of Lancaster Seminary. His life-long interest in adult education makes it most appropriate that this series be dedicated to him. Three other staff members have guided the series through the writing and production stages: The Rev. Jack H. Haney, Project Coordinator for the Kaleidoscope Series, The Rev. Nancy G. Wright, Editor for Kaleidoscope, and Mr. Gene Permé, Marketing Director. As a publishing staff they have provided valuable experience and counsel. Finally, I wish to recognize the creative leadership of Mrs. Jean Vieth, the Seminary Coordinator for the Series, has been active for several years in this educational program at Lancaster.

Peter M. Schmiechen, President
The Lancaster Theological Seminary

Preface

The idea of conversion presented in this study first took shape in the late 1960s, when I found myself struggling with the task of interpreting Paul to college students and at the same time trying to come to terms with the shattering events of American society. To say that it was a troublesome time hardly catches the seriousness of these events. We were as a nation, in spite of all our attempts to prevent it or ignore it, pushed into the terrifying experience of a crisis. What we thought were treasured traditions and centers of value worthy of our loyalty were revealed to be quite fragile, if not destructible. In such a crisis of loss, the overpowering message of Paul about the power and wisdom of God, revealed in the weakness and foolishness of the cross, once more came alive.

Over many years of my life the perspective of crises (in individual life or broad social upheavals) came to be applied to Christian conversion. My vision of conversion as having its genesis in crisis was reenforced by further teaching and shared experience. It then took the form of the course *Becoming a Christian* in the Lancaster Seminary program for laity called Spectrum. Jean Vieth, the coordinator of the Kaleidoscope Series and the former director of Spectrum, encouraged me to develop the idea into this book for the Kaleidoscope series.

I wish to thank the faculty and staff of Mansfield College, Oxford, England, for admission to the college during a four-month study leave in 1989. The Reverend Charles Brock, chaplain, was especially helpful in making available to me the great resources of the college and the university. This sabbatical allowed me to write a draft of the text. I am most grateful for having had this opportunity for study, reflection, and writing and thank the trustees of Lancaster Seminary for granting me such a leave.

The transition from draft to final text was directed by The Reverend Nancy Wright, editor. I wish to thank her for her wise counsel and assistance. She brought to this task the right balance of admonition and encouragement. The initial manuscript and numerous changes were prepared by Mary Lin Siever, whose excellent work supported this project. The editing and rewriting, while often time-consuming and stressful, nevertheless renewed my faith in the dialogic process. After their expression, ideas take shape and grow only in the process of critical reflection with other people. We discover what we want to say only after saying it and receiving the response of others. Each time we think the process of self-expression is complete, we discover it can be enlarged by our life together. My faith in community has been renewed by this writing and reflection process, which illustrates the dynamics of being and becoming, as discussed in the text. The work is now offered to the community of faith. It does indeed reflect my views, but I know that such views will be enlarged and corrected by future dialogue.

The Gift and the Promise

Becoming What We Are in Christ

Chapter 1

Turning

How do we become Christians? What does it mean to have Christian faith? This book will examine the concept of faith from the standpoint of the experience of crisis and reorientation. The assumption is that one becomes a Christian through the discovery that trust has been misplaced and must be redirected toward God. This process has been traditionally called conversion. The crisis and reorientation of conversion, or genuine trust in God, can occur both in individual self-consciousness as well as in societal forms of identity and worth.

A vivid portrayal of conversion, both personal and societal, is given in the first and second chapters of 1 Corinthians. By focusing on these chapters and adding to them an awareness of the dynamics of Paul's own conversion, we can appreciate the depth of a mature human response to the gospel of Christ. This will provide an entry into examination of what such a response means for us today, what individual experiences of conversion we have undergone, or what growth in faith we may want to welcome into our lives.

Paul and the Church at Corinth

Paul was not one of the original disciples but a devout Jew converted to the Christian faith after strongly opposing it. His conversion was probably in the years A.D. 31 or 32. He then spent some ten to fifteen years in the Roman provinces north of Jerusalem. During this period he came to know the disciples and, in the famous confrontation with Peter (Galatians 2:11–14), upheld the principle that gentiles need not first become Jews (that is, fulfill the social, dietary, and moral requirements of the law) before becoming Christians. (Scholars reconstruct the chronology for Paul's life by matching

1

references in the text with known events, as well as by using references to time by Paul himself. Most of the dates are estimates. The chronology used here is that of W. G. Kummel, *Introduction to the New Testament*, rev. ed. [London: SCM Press, Ltd., 1966].)

Firm in his conviction that the gospel was a divine invitation to the gentile world as well as to Israel, Paul set out on his travels around what is now Turkey, Greece, and Rome. He was often accompanied by his friends Barnabas, Titus, and Timothy. Between the years 49 and 52, he spent a year and a half in Corinth, where he succeeded in gathering a church of gentiles and Jews.

Corinth was a commercial city on the narrow strip of land that connects the northern part of Greece with the large land area in the south, known as the Peloponnesus. The city had been completely destroyed and then rebuilt by the Romans a century earlier. Another missionary, Apollos, also spent time in Corinth, and Paul considered him a friend. About two or three years after his stay in Corinth, Paul is in Turkey. There he receives a report from Chloe's people (1 Corinthians 1:11) that the Corinthians are quarreling. There is also some evidence that Paul had made a second trip to Corinth and wrote a letter (now lost), but his efforts had only made things worse. (For more information on Paul see C. K. Barrett, *A Commentary on the First Epistle to the Corinthians*, 2nd ed. [London: Adam and Charles Black, 1971], 1–7.) Paul decides to send Timothy to Corinth and to write a new letter. Before the letter is written, however, a delegation from Corinth arrives with questions to Paul regarding disputed issues. Paul then writes what we now know as 1 Corinthians.

We need to remember that 1 Corinthians is a letter. An essayist writes for a general audience, explains the context and issues, and then proceeds to the substance of the argument. By contrast, the letter writer is quite specific, assuming the readers know the context. Letters tend to move directly to analysis and solutions, without telling us what the problems are. This describes Paul's letter to the Corinthians. Paul wrote the letter about 54 or 55, which makes it one of the earliest parts of the New Testament. (The earliest Gospel, Mark, was not written until A.D. 65 to 70.) Paul had heard and knew the outline of the Gospel (see 1 Corinthians 15), but he did not have access to any written gospel.

Everything we know about Paul and the Corinthian church comes from his letters or the Book of Acts. We are assisted by general knowledge of the social and religious life of first century Greece. But none of these sources gives us a complete description of the situation that inspired this letter. We need to work backward from the letter, using Paul's own descriptions and hints, in order to reconstruct the quarrel to which he devoted much attention and concern.

The Crisis at Corinth

If one catalogues the disputes and questions put to Paul, it is clear that the Corinthian church has problems. Various factions are making counter claims regarding wisdom and authority; there are disputes over marriage and sexual practices, and some have taken their disputes to the civil courts; a debate rages about food consecrated to idols; the Lord's Supper is in controversy; and some have uttered the charge: "Jesus be cursed [12:3]!" And you thought your church had problems!

What concerns Paul the most is the general situation of contending parties. Scholars disagree regarding the number and substance of these parties. That Paul is willing to use the basic vocabulary of the opposition (e.g., the word *wisdom*) to interpret the gospel suggests that the lines of distinction between Paul, the opposition (possibly a form of Hellenistic religion known as Gnosticism), and Hellenistic Judaism are quite fluid. The key, therefore, is not the use of a word, but how it is used.

Most scholars agree that the general shape of the argument in opposition to Paul can be described in the following way: Christianity is a new form of knowledge or wisdom that elevates the recipient to a higher spiritual state. These "spiritual ones" achieve self-realization but, more important, freedom from the restrictions of earthly life, whether these take the form of tradition, rules, or even concern for physical life. The "spiritual ones" are free to do as they please. The earth and our fleshly bodies are seen as the antitheses of the Spirit.

The claim to a new spiritual life is not identical with Gnosticism though it has definite similarities. It certainly is not the problem Paul faces in several other situations, where the opposition consists of strict legalists seeking to impose all of the Jewish social and legal traditions upon the church. Here in Corinth are several groups, each claiming a particular form of wisdom. One group is libertarian, claiming freedom to act as its members please. Another holds that its wisdom is superior to the others'; it claims the names of (and thus identity with) Peter, Apollos, or Paul. Another affirms the exalted Christ as the true spiritual wisdom but disdains the idea that the Christ should be identified with the historical, fleshly Jesus, who suffered death. For this group it is consistent with the affirmation of Christ to say "Jesus be cursed!" (For an explanation of this strange remark see Walter Schmithals, *Gnosticism in Corinth* [Nashville: Abingdon Press, 1971] 125–36; and Birger A. Pearson, *The Pneumatikos-Psychikos Terminology in 1 Corinthians* [Missoula, Montana: Scholars Press, 1973] 23–33.)

Now, it is true that Paul eventually works his way through each dispute and question, but the main concern for Paul is that the competing parties base their views of themselves on claims to special wisdom. To make matters worse, Paul himself is part of the problem. It was Paul who brought to Corinth a message of freedom from the law and a new knowledge of God in Jesus Christ. Paul himself, it appears, either introduced or used the image of wisdom in asserting that Jesus Christ is the "wisdom of God" (see 1:24) that bestows upon the believer a new spiritual life, which is itself a sign of the new age.

Confronting the Cause, Not the Symptoms

The Corinthian situation clearly demands clarification regarding the particular disputes and Paul's own position. Some might think that a brief, sharply worded letter of reprimand from Paul would suffice, since the behavior of the congregation is so outrageous. Would not such a warning, coupled with visits from Timothy and Paul in the near future, serve to calm the storm? That Paul has already tried this course and failed is one reason against another such attempt. More important, Paul's view of human nature requires a more fundamental response. Quarreling, law suits, drunkenness, arrogance, disregard of the weaker members, and even sexual license are symptoms of a basic disorder. Forcing people to change the symptoms will not solve the disorder. Paul makes an assumption that is profound with respect to its insight into human nature and momentous in its impact upon Christian tradition. Paul assumes that human action proceeds out of, and expresses, a person's character or state of being. A phrase more popular today is "Action arises out of one's heart or mind."

In deliberating on his response did Paul recall the saying of Jesus: A good tree bears good fruit and a bad tree bears bad fruit? The general idea that action arises from one's heart is not original with Paul, but it becomes the basis for his answer to the Corinthians. As every parent knows, it is one thing for children to stop fighting in your presence; it is a very different thing for them not to fight when you are away; and it takes a miracle for them to love one another. Only an answer that goes beyond the symptoms to the very being, or the self-consciousness, of those involved will create a solution. But how are the minds and hearts of people changed?

The Cross as the Unveiling of a Crisis

Paul's answer to the crisis is that he must persuade the Corinthians that something is wrong—not just in their symptomatic actions, but at the fundamental level of causes. The problem lies in the personal claims, the reason the Corinthians were making claims, and the necessity that drove them to defend these claims in spite of the negative consequences. In claiming for oneself or one's group what is not one's own, Paul detects something deeply wrong, which is totally opposed to the mind of Christ. Paul discerns that the Corinthian Christians must turn away from their own wisdom *to* the wisdom of God. For this to occur, Paul decides to force a confrontation of the most extreme sort. After the appropriate introductions and a general thanksgiving (1:1–9), Paul chooses to speak of the cross. Only the cross can break through the preoccupation with self and the blindness that prevent the disputing parties from seeing reality. Paul's thesis is that worldly claims to wisdom are destructive and misguided; they cannot produce what they promise. The cross means an end to all such claims.

The Cross of Jesus

To unpack the full meaning of Paul's insights, let us ask a simple question: Who killed Jesus? The immediate answers may be "the Jews," or "the Romans." But for Paul, such answers are too general and miss the point. Jesus was crucified by an opposition that included some fellow Jews (lawyers, teachers, and priests) as well as Roman provincial authorities. But what defines or distinguishes the perspective of those opposed to Jesus? For Paul the answer is people's specific claims to wisdom. Jesus was perceived as a blasphemer and insurrectionist, a threat to religious, social, and political values. He was judged as one who challenged the authority of claims to religious wisdom and political power. The terrifying aspect of the cross (for Paul and all those who have been influenced by him) is that those who crucified Jesus were not underworld criminals. Nor were they seeking to overthrow what we normally call a just and ordered society. To the contrary, Jesus was crucified by those in authority, those endowed with responsibility for preserving and affirming truth and justice. The opposition to him cut across his own people, including the progressive Pharisees and the more conservative Sadducees; his death was imposed by a government that had extended civilization to the ends of the known world. Paul can say with conviction: "None of the rulers of this age understood this [God's plan]; for if they had, they would not have crucified the Lord of glory [2:8]."

The cross creates a radical crisis in understanding about the world and God's purposes for it and for ourselves if—and this is absolutely crucial—one believes that Jesus is the Christ and Lord. If Jesus is the Christ and Lord, then the world's religious and political leaders crucified the wrong person in the defense of their wisdom. Here then is Paul's point: The crucifixion of Jesus reveals that the leaders were not in fact wise; they were misled and could not see God's messenger. It reveals that the leaders were not truly powerful, because while intending to preserve peace and justice, they unjustly put to death the innocent. God uses the weakness and foolishness of Jesus' death to reveal that something is wrong with worldly wisdom and power. Only when God's intentions are acknowledged can we begin to see that Jesus points to a different kind of wisdom.

Paul's Own Conversion

Before we deal with Paul's application of Jesus' cross to the Corinthian church, there is an intermediate link that must be exposed. Paul is able to see the world in terms of Jesus' cross because it had become the center of his own life.

Paul was a Hellenistic Jew, educated in Tarsus and even in Jerusalem under the famous Rabbi Gamaliel (Acts 22:3). He was a Roman citizen, thereby possessing privilege and status. He lived in radical obedience to the law. He not only affirmed the law and made it his claim, but he actively opposed the Christians because of it. Acts 9:1 describes him as "breathing threats and murder against the disciples," and Paul himself refers to his zeal in confronting the Christians (Acts 22:3). He claims to have imprisoned some and given consent to the death of others, including Stephen's.

Paul's conversion is described in three places in Acts (9:1–22; 22:1–21, 26:1–23). While on the way to Damascus in search of followers of Jesus, Paul is confronted by Christ himself. This appearance of the risen Jesus is the basis for Paul's turning, and he repeatedly bases his claim to being an apostle—equal to the disciples who saw the risen Lord—on this encounter. But we need to emphasize that the appearance of Christ has a very specific thematic character: Christ challenges Paul's claim to knowledge and righteousness. A voice says to Paul "Why are you persecuting me?" When Paul asks who is speaking, the voice says, "I am Jesus, whom you are persecuting."

Paul's encounter with Christ unveils foremost that he is in the wrong. Paul's religious zeal is misplaced; he has the blood of Stephen on his hands, even if he did not throw a stone. What Paul took to be correct and necessary is now revealed to him as a form of persecution of the Christ who appears to him. At the most fundamental level, the initial encounter with Christ is the discovery of the meaning of being in opposition to Christ.

Paul's conversion thus becomes his primary experience—both in time and personal significance—for understanding the gospel. Before he writes to the Corinthians about the strange wisdom of God in the cross, Paul has already experienced it in his own life. His former claim to knowledge resulted in conflict and death. His claim to authority resulted in the suffering of the followers of Jesus. Is it any wonder that all three accounts of Paul's conversion in Acts give us the powerful images of light and blindness! Paul is confronted by a light for the purpose of leading others to the light, but he himself is struck blind, and his eyes are only opened three days later. Before he can see, he must be blinded. How different 2 Corinthians 4:6 reads if we understand it against this background: "For it is the God who said, 'Let light shine out of darkness', who has shone in our hearts to give the light of the knowledge of the glory of God in the face of Christ."

Claims to Wisdom

Now we can see why Paul has no trouble connecting the story of the crucifixion of Jesus with the crisis at Corinth. Like Paul, the Corinthians are engaged in persecuting Jesus Christ. Was not Jesus crucified by those who made claims to wisdom and power? In a parallel way, the quarreling at Corinth arises out of claims to wisdom and power. These actions are like the crucifixion of Jesus in two ways. They are destructive to the people and the community, and they are

misguided. The results are contrary to the espoused end results of
wisdom and spiritual power. Just as the actual cross of Jesus is for Paul
a sign of false wisdom and abuse of power by those in authority, so the
quarreling of the Corinthians is a sign of false wisdom and an abuse of
power. In both cases the destructive actions arise out of claims to
wisdom, but in both cases the results are negative. In each case the
cross unveils profound disorder. The cross not only exposes the
contradictory and powerless nature of claims but ultimately is a
discovery that all claims must end.

It should now be clear why Paul chooses to talk about the cross in
writing to the Corinthians. Perhaps we can now reread 1 Corinthians
1:17–31 to understand the repeated play on words Paul uses to break
through to the readers. The following are his major antitheses:

The Wisdom of the World and the Wisdom of God

By *world* Paul does not mean the original created order but the
world of human culture now so caught in alienation and warfare that
it is cut off from God. It no longer knows God or comprehends how to
judge the truth about human relations or God. The "wisdom of God"
refers not to a knowledge internal to God, but to the plan of salvation
for all people determined before all ages (2:7) and made known in
Jesus Christ.

The Standards for Judgment

Worldly wisdom requires signs and wonders (1:22) and seeks
expression in eloquent and plausible words (2:2–4). Is this not the
equivalent of requiring immediate and short-term payoffs (a vindica-
tion of our side) and solutions that increase our positions of wealth
and power over against our neighbors' or enemies'? Signs and wonders
are pleasing to us; those in power determine what is eloquent and
plausible. By contrast, the wisdom of God begins with reconciling
love (the weakness of the cross) and the confession that the crucified
one is Lord (foolishness).

The Consequences

Since worldly wisdom is powerless, it cannot know God; since it
has crucified the Christ, it is misguided, in spite of all its intellectual,
social, and political power. But God, in faithfulness to the divine
love, chooses what is foolish to make foolish the wisdom of the world
(1:20,25,27) and what is weak to overthrow the powerful of the world
(1:25–28).

Boasting As A Sign of Worldly Claims

One form of action is a clear sign of a worldly person's mind and heart: boasting. Worldly wisdom necessitates an endless process of claiming and invariably expresses itself in boasting one's superiority and maturity. By contrast, those who see the cross as a turning point are released from the need to make claims and, therefore, need not boast. Before God and neighbor, they live in the world in the knowledge that saving wisdom and power belong to God.

One Cross—Three Stories

We are now in a position to see that three stories are at work in the first letter to the Corinthians and that they are interacting in the mind of Paul to produce a rich but complex text. The three are the stories of Jesus, of Paul's conversion, and of the crisis of Corinth. Paul interprets Corinth in light of his interpretation of Jesus' crucifixion, which in turn conforms to his personal story. Here are the parallel ideas of the stories.

1. In Jesus' story the antagonists make claims to moral and religious authority in order to preserve tradition and order. The sign of the crisis is the cross.

2. In Paul's story the antagonist is Paul himself, who makes authoritative claims and persecutes the followers of Jesus. The signs of the crisis are the martyred Stephen and the appearance of Jesus, which strikes Paul blind.

3. In Corinth the antagonists are the various factions, all of which make claims to knowledge, moral righteousness, and spiritual freedom. The signs of the crisis are quarrelling, division, and strife.

In all three stories conflict leads to crisis. Each crisis involves suffering and pain. In each crisis God uses suffering to unveil misplaced and counterproductive claims.

The Cross as Symbol of Our Common Experience

In 1 Corinthians 1 and 2 although Paul interprets the Corinthian situation by means of the story of Jesus, we can assume that his own story is on his mind as well, generating the presuppositions of his thought (cf. 1 Corinthians 9:1 and 15:8). This illustrates a pattern of interpretation that has become common in Christian tradition and that we need to employ: the ability to read the story of Jesus in relation to our own personal stories and our social situations. Like Paul, we find ourselves in a three-cornered situation:

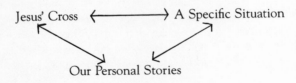

Just as Paul's letters reveal that the three foci always interact, so our attempts to understand the Christian life should involve such three-fold analysis. We are reading 1 Corinthians 1 and 2 in an attempt to understand both the meaning of Jesus Christ and our own lives. The Corinthian situation, Jesus' cross, and our lives thus become the three subjects interacting in this discussion.

Paul is so convinced of the connection between Jesus' cross and the crisis at Corinth that he begins to use the cross as a symbol of a universal experience, which is this: Human suffering and social disorder can be signs that something is wrong. Too often people are so busy claiming wisdom that they are unable to see such problems. The problems then escalate until a crisis occurs. The crisis expresses both the reality of the problems and the contradictions in personal claims. Consider several commonplace examples:

1. We create complex and efficient schedules for parents and children, as expressions of our commitments to careers, home life, education, and recreation. But if in the process the family has little time together, does not the pain of isolation become a cross, an unveiling that perhaps the schedule is not wise?

2. Governments are supposed to be, and claim to be, the agents of a just social order. But when they engage in war, does not the suffering and death of people become a cross, a revealing of the gap between claims and the reality of justice?

3. Social revolutionaries point to injustices and offer solutions they claim lead us to a more perfect order. But when they engage in acts of violence, as for example in terrorist attacks on civilians, does not the pain become a cross, a revealing of the contradiction betweeen claims and reality?

4. A person dies of lung cancer, perhaps due to smoking. Does not

this death become a cross, the unveiling of the falsehood in the claim that smoking will make a person look and feel good?

Those with eyes to see the contradictions in these claims can understand Paul's charge against worldly wisdom. The world claims to value life but causes death, to desire community but perpetuates alienation, to honor law and social order but acts in contrary ways, and to praise the pursuit of happiness but tolerates ever increasing levels of despair. The cross, as a crisis event, has the ability to unveil and expose the contradictions that are part of our world. For Paul, the cross is the way God shatters the false confidence of the world by means of the death of the innocent Jesus. The shame brought upon the wise and strong (1:27) lies in the fact that they are blind to the truth and have employed power in the ways of death. The cross reverses all judgments to reveal that things are not what they seem to be. Nothing becomes something, and something is reduced to nothing. (Or does Paul really mean a nobody becomes a somebody and the somebodies of the world become nobodies?) The final reversal is that the divine foolishness and weakness become the power of salvation (1:18). But the Corinthians cannot see this, because they claim that wisdom and power arise in themselves. So the cross must be a word of judgment that destroys every false claim, so that all claims will be based in God alone. The cross is always a crisis that can be a turning point.

Summary

Our analysis of Paul's debate with the Corinthians has focused on several crucial themes. (1) Paul resolves to deal with the *minds and hearts* of the readers and not simply their *actions*, because he is persuaded that actions arise out of the way people define themselves and see the world. (2) Paul encounters a *worldly wisdom* that denies any connection with the historical Jesus who suffered and died. It expresses itself in *claims* to spiritual maturity and unrestricted freedom. (3) Paul contrasts such worldly wisdom with the *wisdom of God* revealed in the crucified Jesus. The gospel is therefore portrayed as the *foolishness and weakness* of God, whereby God uses the *cross* to reveal the futility of worldly wisdom. Paul's view is a theology of the cross: The cross unveils the destructive nature of our claims, but it also makes possible a turning away from our claims. In the next chapter we shall complete our analysis of the nature of worldly claims to wisdom and discuss Paul's understanding of the gospel as a gift.

Issues for Reflection and Discussion

1. Review the key words (italicized) in the summary. How would you define the opposition and Paul's position? Why is the gospel foolishness and weakness? Why does God use such foolishness and weakness?

2. Do you see any claims to worldly wisdom in our society? Consider several different kinds. Why do they have such appeal?

3. Do you think the cross exposes a crisis? Have you ever faced a crisis that became a cross event in Paul's sense? What were your reactions and feelings? How was the matter resolved?

4. In today's newspaper, do you find any claims being made? Do you see reports on any crises that represent a cross event?

5. Do you see the cross in the church sanctuary in a new light after reading Paul? Why is it important for the church to keep its eyes on the cross?

Chapter 2

The Gift

The Christian faith affirms that new life is, from first to last, a gift. It is even a debated issue whether we turn to the gift or are ourselves turned to it by a gracious Presence. Paul desperately wants to share with the Corinthians the gift of new life, the wondrous love that inspires it, and the faithful Spirit that actualizes it in our lives. But the meaning and value of any gift are dependent upon the needs and standards of the recipient. The Corinthians undervalue and misunderstand the gift of Christ because of their standards of what is true and powerful. The wondrous gift has been presented, but it becomes the occasion for quarreling and disorder. Could a more striking contradiction ever be found!

Paul's immediate goal is to change the behavior of the Corinthians. It is self-evident to him that the gift of Christ brings love and peace rather than quarrels and disorder. But he has discovered that actions proceed out of a person's mind and heart. It is naive to ask people to replace quarrels with friendship, boasting with humility, self-centeredness with love if people feel compelled to act the way they do. The disorderly folk in Corinth need to know why they should change their behavior. Even more crucial, their minds and hearts must first be changed! The problem Paul faces can be illustrated in a diagram:

State of Mind/Heart	*Actions*
Worldly Wisdom (B)	Quarrels and boasting (A)
Christian Wisdom (C)	Love and Humility (D)

One's immediate reaction to the situation at Corinth point **A** might be to try to change the actions, to move people directly from **A** to **D**. Paul has tried this and failed. He has discovered that there are no short cuts; he must take the long way around, from **A** to **B** to **C** to **D**. Therefore, his initial strategy has been to attack point **B**, the worldly wisdom that motivates the negative action. This he has done by his argument against claims, that the cross exposes the futility of claims based on worldly standards.

The long range strategy, however, is directed toward point **C** and ultimately point **D**. By the power of God, the foolishness of the cross becomes the occasion for a turning to a new mind and heart, which Paul aptly calls the "mind of Christ" (2:16). Only the new mind of Christ can liberate us from the destructive power of claims based on worldly standards. This new mind is not a human invention, nor an accomplishemnt, nor a possession to be controlled. It is a gift that enables the person to become and be fully human: to care for others, to live humbly, and to make peace. It is the ability to love.

Paul wants to speak of the gift, but instead he must talk about "turning," or becoming, to people who already profess to being in Christ. Did they not turn enough, take a wrong turn, or even make a reverse turn after the original turning? Whatever the case, Paul's letter has demonstrated the connections between claims and the human inability to turn to the gift. Some of these connections need to be explored, lest we, too, undervalue the gift of Christ or misunderstand it.

Claims as Barriers to Receiving the Gift

The Origin of Claiming

Why do human beings become so involved in claiming? In terms of the biblical perspective, humanity is created in the image of God. This affirms that while we are finite, physical creatures like all other living things, we are beings capable of free expression and responsiveness to other humans and to God. It is in this sense that we are spiritual—not as divine or nonfleshly creatures—but as personal beings. The image of God is not one function (such as reason, artistic expression, or will) that we carry within us. Rather it is the empowerment of all of these aspects in a unified consciousness capable of a personal life lived with and for other persons and the world.

As finite, self-conscious creatures, we have needs common to all living things. But these needs are met in ways reflecting our creativity, our remembrance of the past, and our values. For example, we could meet all our nutritional needs with three servings per day of a fortified porridge. But we would soon rebel. We do not simply consume food but meet the physical need of hunger in ways reflecting cultural, social, religious, economic, and individual values. To further compli- cate matters, we have needs unique to our spirit-filled consciousness. Meaning and value, freedom and power, beauty and moral goodness are all as essential to being human as is biological survival. As a Madison Avenue promotion says: "We want to succeed, not just survive." Success can be making and defending claims to value or power and in this sense is a legitimate expression of our humanity. Our identity, worth, and meaning are shaped by our development in time and place as well as our own actions and decisions. We are what we claim, for the claims represent our inherited personal identity as well as the work of our own lives. We would cease to be human if we were not concerned about standards of value and levels of power that enable us to realize the highest forms of human life.

But where then did things go wrong for the Corinthians? What is problematic in our claiming? When we rely again upon the biblical view, we recognize that we claim too much for ourselves and certain things and, in some cases, claim the wrong thing. We err when we turn our legitimate needs into idols. The following examples illustrate this point:

1. In the twentieth century our need for meaning in the developed First World has resulted in endless consumption. This entails the use of other people (and the environment) for our purposes and the claim of knowing all we need to know.

2. Our need for power has become a drive to rule over others and the Earth. We live in the illusion that we are independent or self- sufficient.

3. Our need for goodness has produced claims to moral and social superiority and the defensive denial of any imperfection.

Is it any wonder that the sensitive person reading the daily newspaper may catch glimpses of a world out of control! People, knowledge, technology, things, and the Earth itself are abused and destroyed in the name of the excessive claims of human beings. The limits of this view are revealed by contrasting images. The Bible affirms that only God knows all things, is almighty, and is perfectly good. To provide one instance, Genesis 3 reveals that to claim too much or the wrong thing is to tell a lie.

The Consequences of Our Claims

When human beings claim too much or the wrong thing, consequences invariably follow. We will describe four here.

First, to claim omniscience or perfection is to create an illusion or pretense. It is to make an idol of ourselves, to pretend we are not flesh and blood. When this occurs we cut ourselves off from God and other human beings. Indeed, it is impossible to live with people who wish to be all powerful (to control things) or who claim perfection (to be always right). Not only do we shy away from such conceit, we fear it because it threatens our physical and spiritual well-being.

Second, those who claim too much fall victim to their own illusions. The compulsion to excess becomes habitual and ultimately confines them in a world of illusory claims. The compulsory nature of this pattern is often described with words such as sickness, bondage, blindness, or being lost.

Modern social sciences have emphasized the power of culture to shape and control the individual. The extreme form of this view affirms that we are totally the products of a vast network of forces that condition us. We need not take this extreme view in order to see connections between our modern awareness of social conditioning and Paul's notion of bondage to worldly standards. Herein lies a paradox that few can unravel: We appear simultaneously to be the victims and the creators of our own bondage. We grow up in a world already at war, an environment already polluted, and in communities already content with a multitude of sins. At the same time, we initiate our own claims, willingly adopt the current claims, and invent some of our own. What we inherit and what we create merge into a network of claims that imprison us.

Third, those who make their identity and worth rest upon their claims are unable to deal in a free or creative way with reality. When problems (e.g., suffering, accidents, errors) occur, those who claim too much are unable to acknowledge responsibility or propose a real solution, because either response would require a revision in the claim. The problem is, therefore, either avoided, denied, or rationalized.

Consider these examples. The first is a problem denied. Chicago's illustrious mayor in the 1960s and 70s, Richard J. Daley, was fond of declaring that there are no ghettos in Chicago. One can imagine that this statement would hardly be believable to Blacks, Hispanics, Asians, Native Americans, or other definable minorities. To whom was the mayor speaking? To white people, of course! The statement was intended to deny a criticism of the city and reassert the majority claim that Chicago is a good, fair, and law-abiding city.

An example of a problem avoided is the often stated comment: "Street people choose to live that way." Now while some street people may be in flight from the confinement of the social patterns of the majority, many of them are alone, marginally mentally deficient, or ill. We also cannot rationalize away the serious problems of unemployment, shortage of low-income housing, poor education, drug addiction, and the great deal of personal distress in a harsh world. The purpose of the comment is to grant absolution to the person who does not want to be concerned with the problems in urban America.

A final example, of a problem rationalized, occurred in the late 1960s when the U.S. National Guard opened fire on protesters at Kent State University, Ohio. When the news arrived at a public library in an area four hundred miles away, two reactions were initially expressed: (1) it can't be true; (2) if it did happen, the students must have deserved it. Consider the reactions, which were made without any supporting information or evidence. The hearers apparently received the news as a threat to their own recognized identity and worth. Their defense against this threat was, in the first instance, denial—"things like that don't happen in America." Their second reaction was to affirm that if the report was true, the students must have done something wrong because our government only does what is right.

Fourth, we can return to the question raised in the previous chapter: Is a cross needed to break through the defenses of the claims? It would be strange for me as an educator to respond by saying that rational discussion is entirely unable to change hearts and minds. But my commitment to education includes what many have called Christian realism. Words in an abstract or theoretical form seldom are capable of piercing human defence mechanisms, but words can point to the reality of our experience and the consequences of our actions. In general, change is precipitated by events; that is, the reality and power of new experience appears to be more capable than reasoning of overcoming claims based on prior experience.

An amazing example of this comes from Northern Ireland. In 1988, a Protestant high school girl resolved to oppose the killing there by arranging a meeting of Protestant and Catholic students. She and her friends had never met a Catholic! To their surprise, they discovered that Catholic students were like and unlike themselves. The action by the student was a courageous act, going against all that she had received in the culture of Protestant claims. Could she have persuaded through rational debate her Protestant classmates of a common humanity shared with Catholics? Probably not. Her classmates had to experience the other students in order to acknowledge the truth of a shared humanity. In her case, it took the crisis of senseless killing to cause her to break out of the cycle of blood vengeance.

Christian faith affirms human rationality, but it also sees the human as more than a neutral thinking machine. We are creatures of physical needs and drives, shaped by centuries of language and culture, each of us struggling in his or her own way to find meaning and worth in a complex world. We are as much creatures of love as we are dispassionate computers. We do, in fact, reason out of our love and hate. We reason for our claims as much as we reason against our claims. Thus, while not an absolute rule, it often takes the crisis of a cross to awaken us to the honest recognition that something is wrong.

As suggested in chapter 1, a cross is a symbol that something is wrong. While a cross may be present in every crisis involving suffering and alienation, not everyone sees the cross in such an event. In fact, the most demonic form of our worldly wisdom is the pretension that a crisis contains no suffering, or even that nothing is wrong. So, for example, in June, 1989, after the student demonstrations in Beijing, the Chinese government sought to avoid seeing the crisis as a cross event by denying that any students were killed. Although not every crisis becomes an experience of the cross or a turning from worldly wisdom to the gift, every crisis may be the occasion for experiencing the cross as both judgment and gift.

The Loss of Our Claims

In our analysis of claims, there is one last subject to confront: What happens to a person when you take away his or her claims? This analysis of the origin and significance of claims is carried out in order to understand just why claims are so hard to give up and why the turning to God's gift is traumatic. It should therefore be evident that to ask for a person to give up claims is in effect to remove all the worldly things that define the person's identity and worth. It is quite correct to use images of being stripped naked, or of being destroyed, or of experiencing a death. Claims are the way we order society and our individual lives; they are part of our personal identity. We have devoted years to achieving certain goals that meet personal and social standards. To remove all these is to be devalued; it is, in effect, to become nothing. To discover oneself in a state of wrong or meaninglessness is a terrifying thing. Is it any wonder, then, that we resist with such energy and passion the criticism against our claims!

But now a word of caution. Just when we begin to understand how our legitimate needs and desires are converted into something that is destructive, we need to keep clear the distinction between the legitimate needs and their pretentious forms. If the distinction is lost, then we end up declaring that all of human life is inherently evil and that there is no solution to our predicament. Such a view has prompted some Christians to adopt an ascetic practice or even the very same Hellenistic views hovering around the debate in Corinth. World-denying attitudes and practices were common in the ancient world and have reappeared in every age. These denials of worldly knowledge and human needs, such as sexuality, art, music, dance, or certain food and drink, have invariably given Christianity a sorrowful mood and a moralistic mind-set. They have also produced a vigorous reaction that sees Christianity as the problem.

A well-known passage in the Bible illustrates the confusion and the protest. In Genesis 3, the admonition not to eat of the tree of the knowledge of good and evil is often interpreted as a command to avoid knowledge. God is, in this interpretation, seen as willing childlike dependence, ignorance, and submissiveness. This argument concludes that we must rightfully rebel from this tyrant God in order to achieve true humanity. In actuality this passage is a prohibition against claiming to be like God, since only God knows all things (that is, good and evil). It is not our humanity that is denied but the pretense and illusion that are the very loss of humanity. Applied to the Corinthians, this Genesis claim means that it is not knowledge per se that is their problem, nor the need for identity and worth, but the way they make claims about this knowledge, identity, and worth. What is wrong is lack of humility before God and others.

The Gift

When the cross event does occur, two reactions are common. On the one hand, a person can easily descend into despair at the loss of the claims that bring meaning and pride to existence. Persons hurt in love easily become cautious about all relationships. Persons whose political ideals are shattered by lies and scandals withdraw their interest and become cynical.

On the other hand, when faced by the terrifying loss of value, some persons ask the question of positive action: "What shall we do?" I call this the revolutionary question, for the words *revolution* and *conversion* share the common root of *turning*. In the Book of Acts, Peter delivers a powerful sermon that totally convicts the audience of being in need of salvation. The listeners are struck down by the discovery of their emptiness before the preaching of the cross. Their question is simply: "Brethren, what shall we do [Acts 2:37]?" The same occurs in Paul's conversion, as reported in Acts 22:10: When Paul is overwhelmed by the knowledge of his misguided zeal, he asks, "What shall I do, Lord?"

In a real sense the revolutionary impulse is the desire to reclothe the naked self, to reconstruct levels of meaning, to right the wrong done so that value can again be affirmed. It is inherent in the human spirit to want to create a new world of meaning and value. It is significant that when Jesus announces the coming of a revolution ("The time is fulfilled, the Kingdom of God is at hand") he also gives to the listener the answer to the question of what should be done: "Repent, and believe in the gospel [Mark 1:15]."

Is Paul aware of the gravity of his attack upon the Corinthians? Of course, because he himself experienced the terrifying loss of his own personal claims. But he does not hold back one bit. He goes to the very heart of their claims and exposes them as foolish and powerless. He even speaks in the most personal terms: they are not wise, powerful, or of noble birth (1 Corinthians 1:26). The only thing that prevents such an attack from being totally destructive is the fact that Paul clearly intends it as the turning point toward receiving the gift. God uses the foolish, the weak, those low and despised, to reveal the salvation of all people. There is a new value and a new truth revealed the moment we lose what the world values and claims as truth. But the new value is not a reconstruction by our hands but the gift of God in Jesus Christ. To those locked into a world of competing claims about goodness and power, the cross is a word of judgment. But to those who have received the cross as a turning to God, the cross is the instrument of new life. Everything that we say about the new life must express one theme: It is a gift from a gracious God.

The Nature of the Gift

Let us outline in broad terms the scope of this gift. In sum, it is the development of a new personal identity, lived out in community, and sustained by the mind of Christ.

The new identity and standing before God. Those outside the realm of the gift define themselves according to their worldly status and the product of their achievements. Those who see the cross as the power of salvation define themselves by God's declaration: You are claimed and loved as a son or daughter of God; you are of worth and are eternally named by God. This declaration is trustworthy and secure, because it rests not on who we are or on what we have done or will do in the future but on the eternal love of God. This obviously involves forgiveness of sin; but, even more, it means that we are reconciled to God because God wills that the separation between us and God should end. Paul is bold to speak in such decisive terms, because the gift is offered to Jew and gentile. God wills life for all people.

The community of God. Those who turn to receive the gift are reconciled to one another and given membership in a new community, not on the basis of worldly standards and claims regarding strength, knowledge, or goodness, but on the basis that God names us one people and wills us to be united. The fact that we as individuals are different and do not agree on many things is, of course, relevant. But our differences and disagreements are not fatal to our membership or the existence of the faith community. This singularity of spirit is seldom realized as we go about creating congregations based on common ties and a set of shared views on life. However, the actual community of God is not a voluntary association of like-minded people but those gathered by Christ, who is the sign of the gift. Christ is the center of the community. It is Christ who unites all the members in spite of their differences. This bonding does not deny or destroy the uniqueness of individuals or gloss over serious differences. Instead, it places the differences in a new context: the presence of a gracious God who wills that we spend the rest of our lives being formed by reconciling love. It is in this sense that the margins, or minority groups, are included in community, because the community does not belong to the majority but to the center, who is Christ.

The mind of Christ. Paul makes it clear in 1 Corinthians 15 that the gospel he received is the foundation for his thought. But when he describes the new life, he is forced to create a new set of terms to express this new reality. Those who have a new identity and standing in the community no longer live alone. They are members of the "body of Christ." They have opened their lives to the Spirit of God. They are "in the Spirit" and the Spirit is in them (2:10–13); in this sense they are truly wise. They are empowered to think and act not according to their own will but the will of God. Since Paul knows that such a statement can mean many things, he is quick to identify the new spiritual person with the concrete Jesus Christ. To be in the Spirit is to be in Christ. In this way Paul makes clear that the new spiritual life finds Christ-centered expressions: faith, hope, and love. In contrast to claims to knowledge, prophecy, and speaking in tongues, the Christian trusts in (has faith in) God and accepts the limitations of knowledge (13:9). Instead of claiming perfection or fullness of the spiritual life, the Christian lives in hope. He or she accepts the promises of God and rests secure in them for the future. Finally, instead of perpetual concern for self—through accumulation of possessions or seeking personal satisfaction at the expense of others—the Christian is able to love. The mind of Christ—trusting in God, hoping for God's realm, and engaging in works of love—is the form of the spiritual life bestowed upon the community of God.

The Consequences of the Gift

There are three future consequences of a life conformed to the gift of Christ. These are freedom, joy, and gratitude. It would surprise the reader if we did not list first "freedom from claims" as a consequence of receiving the gift of Christ. For a devoutly religious person who feels the overwhelming obligation of the moral life, this freedom is no small matter. It means we are released from the need to make claims about ourselves in order to guarantee our worth and from the need to protect ourselves from claims against us. If God has claimed us in spite of what or who we are, then no judgment can sting or wound. But the freedom Paul announces extends beyond the law. Christ is the power of God freeing us from the powers of evil, from oppressive rulers of this world, and ultimately from death itself. We are free, however, to be a part of the community of God—not to be a tyrant or live for ourselves. Freedom is the liberation from the frantic demand to prove ourselves; it is also the call to be human in an inhuman world.

Another sign of the mind of Christ is joy, since the one who has received the gift rejoices in the knowledge of his or her identity before God and friendship with the people of God. The mood of Christmas and Easter is joy. To be sure, Advent calls us to hope, and Lent calls us to remember the brokenness of the world. But both Advent and

Lent conclude with the announcement of God's surprising work of salvation.

Finally, gratitude marks the Christian life. A Lutheran hymn begins with the following line:

> O rejoice ye Christians loudly, for our joy has now begun,
> Wondrous things our God has done.

It then concludes—and rightly so—with this stanza:

> Lord how shall I thank thee rightly?
> I acknowledge that by thee, I am saved eternally.

Christian life is ultimately a life of joyous gratitude. If it is not, then we do not understand the gift. Whatever we do, whether works of service or worship of God, is to be done out of gratitude. Whatever we think about God must always begin with the gift and end with grateful praise.

Summary

Our analysis of 1 Corinthians 1 and 2 has brought us to several conclusions: (1) The conflict between Paul and the Corinthians is a conflict about *claims:* the *wisdom of the world* revealed in spiritual pride and the abuse of freedom, and the *wisdom of God* revealed in the *cross.* (2) Claims originate in our quest for identity and worth and are crippling in their *consequences* when we claim too much. Because claims relate directly to essential needs of human beings, they are defended with energy, and their *loss* is potentially very distressing. (3) The gospel is defined as a *crisis* involving a cross that allows us to *turn* to the *gift* of Christ. This gift offers a new identity in the community of God sustained by the mind of Christ. (4) *The mind of Christ* expresses itself in faith, hope, and love, and its consequences are freedom, joy, and gratitude. (5) Becoming Christian is, therefore, a *process of turning* to new identity and worth received as a gift. It involves a total reorientation of the self.

Issues for Reflection and Discussion

1. Review the key words in the summary. Has your understanding of them changed since the close of chapter 1?

2. Why is it important to describe the gospel as a gift rather than a worldly claim? Does the analysis of the gift describe your understanding of Christian life?

3. The best test of our understanding of concepts is our ability to use them. Where do you see claims, the consequences of claims, and the defense of claims in your own life?

Chapter 3

Expanding Our View
of Faith

In American culture Christian faith is easily confined to one sector of our lives called the personal. Discussions about faith and conversion are then understood in terms of individual life and related to personal meaning, self-acceptance, sickness, and death. Although the new life in Christ is rooted in the personal, it cannot be confined to the individual life. This chapter expands the concepts of faith, crisis, and turning, in order to understand them in the context of the full range of human social experience.

Our focus is the view of faith developed by H. Richard Niebuhr in *Radical Monotheism and Western Culture* (New York: Harper and Brothers, 1960). Niebuhr was born in 1894, the son of a pastor in the Evangelical Synod of North America. (These churches merged with the German Reformed Church in 1934 to form the Evangelical and Reformed Church, and in turn entered the United Church of Christ in 1957.) After serving as President of Elmhurst College and teaching at Eden Theological Seminary, Niebuhr taught theology and ethics at Yale Divinity School until his death in 1962. For many decades he was a leading American theologian who continues to be influential through present generations of students.

Human Experience as an Expression of Faith

Niebuhr's view of faith and God can be summarized for our purposes under five general headings. These are faith, the distinction among three types of faith, the emergence of radical monotheism, conversion to monotheism, and the unity of God and the unity of the self.

Faith

On the very first page of *Radical Monotheism and Western Culture*, Niebuhr announces that he wishes to speak of faith and that faith is to be distinguished from religion. This announcement is absolutely decisive in shaping the way he will develop the subject. Niebuhr presents an alternative to a long tradition in the modern age that confines faith to religion and then separates religion into the margins of serious intellectual and social discussion. For Niebuhr faith is natural and necessary to being human; it appears in every realm of human endeavor. It obviously appears in religion, but it also is at the heart of political, economic, and moral systems. We "believe" in democracy, the stock market reacts to a "lack of confidence," and people debate the issue of abortion on the basis of their "commitment" to various values.

The universality of faith leads Niebuhr to affirm the interrelation of faith and reason (pp. 13–16). Here again Niebuhr is working against much of the common wisdom of the modern world. Instead of defining faith and reason as opposites, which leads to the notion of an irrational faith versus a scientific and objective reason, Niebuhr affirms the interconnection of the two. All reasoning proceeds from some starting point that is accepted on trust; conversely, reason is employed to examine and criticize acts of trust. There is no reasoning without faith, and there is seldom a faith that does not reflect on itself.

These introductory assumptions lead Niebuhr to define faith as trust and loyalty (pp. 16–21). Faith has a twofold rhythm: it is trust or confidence in whatever gives value to the person, and it is loyalty to a cause. Trust includes a passive element, in that a person gives trust usually only to someone or something that has proven trustworthy. By contrast, loyalty is a more active response of the person to a cause that is valuable.

To uncover the universal character of faith, Niebuhr defines the object of trust and loyalty as a center of value (p. 18). As such, a center of value appears in the nation, the economy or stock market, one's race, the self, or any cause espoused by the self. All these are objects of trust and loyalty and have many of the characteristics of religious faith in God.

Types of Faith

Niebuhr next turns to the distinction between three types of faith.

In each the value center is different, and this difference determines the shape of faith as well.

The first type of faith is polytheism. *Polytheism* is the traditional term we use to describe belief in many gods. Niebuhr uses it for any situation where faith is directed toward many value centers (pp. 28–31). In some cases there is a hierarchy, with one high God or value center; in other cases there is simply a recognition of random diversity. Faith is parceled out to many objects of trust and loyalty.

A second type of faith is henotheism, a word that means one God (pp. 24–28). While henotheism appears similar to monotheism, it is quite different. Henotheism asks for a total and absolute commitment to one thing or group, even though it recognizes other things or people. As a consequence, henotheistic faith always produces conflict among groups or nations. Niebuhr believed that henotheism is the chief threat to Christianity in the modern age, where political, economic, and racial warfare has been dominant. Writing at midcentury, Niebuhr could point to the imperial pretensions of Nazi Germany or Japan as examples. But any social tyranny illustrates henotheism, be it a dictatorship, a religion, or racism.

Nationalism illustrates Niebuhr's point about henotheism. Nationalism becomes tyrannical in its demand that all trust and loyalty be given to one's own nation. This goes beyond the normal expectation of loyalty to country. It demands the denial of any loyalty to other people or to international values. Other nations may be deceived, exploited, conquered, or destroyed, since "they" possess no value except in their ability to contribute to "our" welfare. Nationalism denies that people are answerable to a higher allegiance, whether humanity or God.

The third type of faith is monotheism. Monotheism affirms one God. It is for Niebuhr radical in its twofold claim: that the one God is the source of all things *and* that the one God is good. This twofold claim gives monotheism its critical power. On the one hand, it challenges every center of value that is less than God (p. 32). Monotheism dethrones any person or thing that claims to be the highest center of value. Like revolutions that topple the statues of dictators, monotheism challenges all tyrants in the name of the Lord of heaven and earth, the Almighty and Holy One. On the other hand, monotheism is radical in its insistence that whatever exists is of value because it has been created by the God who is good.

Niebuhr is quite aware that monotheism is not self-evident or our usual form of faith (pp. 32–33). Monotheism is constantly threatened by trust and loyalty directed toward partial or limited causes, which, like the Old Testament golden calf, are visible and of our making. But Niebuhr is unrelenting in his insistence that monotheism will settle for nothing less than the inclusion of all people and things into our realm of value, against every closed and exclusive claim. In a soft but serious tone, Niebuhr concludes by criticizing Albert Schweitzer, who affirmed reverence for life as a general faith (pp. 36–37). To be sure, life is to be valued, but can we exclude all nonliving things? Radical monotheism affirms that God is God alone, the Creator of all things.

The Emergence of Radical Monothism

While Niebuhr is unwilling to rule out the presence of monotheism in other times and places, he affirms the confessions of Jews and Christians that such a faith has appeared in Israel and in Jesus Christ (pp. 40–42). Since monotheism is a matter of trust and loyalty in the living God, revelation is not a series of propositions (i.e., general ideas or summary doctrines) but is those events that demonstrate loyalty and disclose a cause (pp. 42–43). Using the experience of Moses, Niebuhr describes three characteristics of the encounter with God: God is revealed as the One above all earthly powers; the Almighty One is trustworthy and faithful; Moses is called to decide for God's cause. In the life of Jesus, all three characteristics are continually present. Jesus simultaneously discloses the goodness of the Almighty God and calls people to affirm God's Rule as the goal for their lives. Jesus is both the incarnation of God in the world, demonstrating the faithfulness of God, and the embodiment of true humanity, demonstrating what constitutes a trustful and loyal response to the Rule of God.

Conversion to Monotheism

Given the multiple ways in which we express our trust and loyalty in pluralism and the exclusiveness of henotheism, it is obvious that becoming a monotheist is a difficult process. It involves the displacement of one or many centers of value for that One who is above all and the source of all. Moreover, it requires the experience over time that this One is trustworthy and, in fact, good. Only when we are convinced of a faithfulness and goodness directed toward us in all things are we able to trust this One and name God as our Creator and Savior.

But this breakthrough is just the beginning of the process, because it requires the transformation of our faith. Now all things, people, roles, and relations must be seen as within covenant relations, subject to the rule of this faithful God (p. 42). The history of Israel and the brief glimpse of the church at Corinth reveal the struggle involved in this transformation.

The Unity of God and the Unity of the Self

There is one intriguing corollary to Niebuhr's view that bears on the process of becoming Christian (pp. 30–31, 44–48). Niebuhr argues that revelation is the disclosure of a faithful self. To believe in God is to trust and be loyal to that personal One, whose faithfulness is disclosed throughout all of life's events, in spite of confusion and suffering. From this experience, Niebuhr draws a conclusion regarding personal identity. Our ability to integrate the many dimensions of our lives and reconcile conflicting experiences is directly related to the integration of divine intentionality. The unity of the one divine Person opens the way for us to become integrated as faithful and loyal agents. To believe that God is one is, therefore, not an abstract affirmation, but a confession that makes possible a redefinition of the person who trusts in such a God.

Expanding Our Perspective on Faith and Turning

There are five areas in which Niebuhr's view enlarges our perspective. They help elucidate the nature of crisis, cross, and turning to receive the gift of Christ.

Faith As An Essential Human Activity

Niebuhr's definition of faith liberates religious faith from confinement to one area of life and places it in the midst of the totality of human trust and loyalty. People respect one another, live together in families, buy stock, believe the newspaper, enlist in military service, fly in airplanes, allow surgeons to operate, and place their savings in banks—all on the basis of trust and loyalty. Human beings are creatures of faith, determining by experience what is trustworthy and committing themselves to causes.

What we have called claiming is part of this faith-giving process. Our claims to worth and meaning are constructed upon a network of individual acts of trust and loyalty. We have staked out lives on claims because we believe them to be trustworthy; we have made commitments to causes. Consider your weekly calendar, or the advertisements in the newspaper, or your favorite magazine. Each day we are obligated and invited to trust and be loyal to claims regarding truth, value, and power. Our discussion of faith in God must always be in the context of the human process of being faithful and making claims.

The Crisis of Multiple Forms of Faith

If we are creatures of trust and loyalty, we must then recognize that we have multiple forms of faith and claims. That these are quite different in kind and level of commitment is to be expected. A normal, healthy life involves balancing and integrating many acts of trust and loyalty without compromise or confusion. Consider the family. A married person has a relationship to spouse, children, parents, grandparents, and siblings, as well as to other relatives. These relationships vary in the kind of claims they make upon us and what we make upon them. When we acknowledge that the world of family relations is only one part of the totality of a person's life, then each human being becomes an amazing conductor and organizer of relations of trust and loyalty.

The balancing of multiple claims is not always perfect or peaceful. Conflict arises because of the expansive nature of our claims. We claim too much or are subject to excessive claims: Shall I work tonight or spend time with the family? Shall I make all the money I can, regardless of how, or shall I be honest? Should the children defend themselves from bullies or refrain from fighting? In defense of the nation, may governments deny human rights? Human life is a catalogue of clashes between conflicting claims. In these conflicts two types of crisis frequently occur, and each may become an occasion for turning to receive the gift of Christ.

The first type of crisis is *collision*. When the claims conflict and require resolution, either one claim or the other must rule, or a compromise must be found that represents a new and higher claim. In the former, one claim wins out: Either I have Thanksgiving dinner at my house or at Mother's! Either I take the job in another city or I don't! Either I vote for this candidate or the other! On the surface, a simple choice appears to resolve the issue, but as we well know, there are probably other unresolved issues that we must face. Who lost in the decision? What are the short- and long-term consequences of one side's gaining the decision?

In the case of compromise regarding colliding claims, a decision is made for a third alternative, one that expresses the interests of both sides. When we recognize that the other side has a valid claim, we move to a higher level of resolution, where both sides find some degree of satisfaction.

In both cases—the either/or situation or the strategy of compromise—the crisis occurs because something is wrong with the claims. The collision of interests reveals a fracture in the human community that cries out for healing.

The second type of crisis experience that occurs in the face of conflicting claims is *an awareness of loss.* One claim is revealed to be unworthy of our trust. Consider these examples: (a) your corporation, or employer, asks you to do something dishonest; (b) an elected figure is exposed as a liar or thief; (c) the government turns out to be the chief polluter of a particular environment. In these examples we find that the persons and organizations we trusted are not worthy of our trust. We had been loyal to them, made sacrifices for them, but we discover the trust was misplaced. This party is not capable of providing a cause for our life that is fulfilling and honorable. Here is loss. What will become of our trust? Will it be lost forever in cynicism, transferred to another but equally frail value center, or directed toward what is truly trustworthy?

In cases of collision and loss, we find ourselves forced to reevaluate our claims. The crisis requires a change or reassignment in our trust and loyalty. There is a turning away from something to something more worthy. Most important is the fact that the change occurs because of the press of events. Something happens that pushes us out of a comfortable situation in which everything was balanced and in order. We are literally forced to see that the claims are contradictory and require a new approach, to see that the value center has lost its power. This is the experience of the void created by every cross-filled crisis. It is seldom verbalized in the language of this book. More often it finds expression in frustration, repressed anger, or emotional distress. In the public sector it finds expression in social conflict, acts of protest, and physical violence.

Faith in God as the Turning

If God alone is God, then faith in such a God requires a reappraisal of all of our acts of faith. Faith in the one, holy God is forever a crisis; our trust and loyalty are tested, redefined, and redirected.

The First Commandment makes clear the terms for life in the presence of God: "I am the Lord your God, who brought you out of the land of Egypt, out of the house of bondage. You shall have no

other gods before me [Deut. 5:6–7]." Restated in the positive formula-
tion of the Shema: "The Lord our God is one Lord; and you shall love
the Lord your God with all your heart, and with all your soul, and
with all your might [Deut. 6:4–5]." Just as in ancient Israel God was
the destroyer of idols, so for us today God judges our presumptuous
claims. This critique is as often a forerunner to our turning as it is a
consequence of our turning. A new situation, taking the form of a
crisis, calls into question our identity and worth.

In this context it may be helpful to view many of the well-known
sayings and deeds of Jesus as acts that precipitates a crisis, that lead to
a turning. In numerous instances Jesus creates a collision with current
claims:

• "No one can serve two masters; . . . You cannot serve God and
mammon [Matt. 6:24]."
• To the man overly committed to his possessions, Jesus said: "You
lack one thing: go, sell all that you have, and give it to the poor, and
you will have treasure in heaven; and come, follow me [Mark 10:21]."
• To disciples desiring power and authority, Jesus said: "But it shall
not be so among you; but whoever would be great among you must be
your servant [Mark 10:43]."
• In another context Jesus asked his disciples: "Who do men say that I
am?" After hearing their responses, Jesus confronts them: "But who
do you say that I am [Mark 8:28–29]?" Not only must the claims
about Jesus be sorted out, but the disciples must speak for themselves
and not simply rely upon the confessions of others.
• In casting out demons, the power of God collides with demonic
power, raising questions about how we shall assess the current balance
between good and evil.

We can also relate the experience of the loss of claims (that is, the
discovery of their inadequacy) to Jesus' sayings and actions. Here we
see that Jesus creates a sense of loss (that is, he destroys confidence in
limited centers of value) as well as responds to people who already
experience the loss:

• The inadequacy of the legal tradition is revealed repeatedly: "You
have heard that it was said. . . . But I say to you . . . [Matthew 5:27–
28]."
• Jesus heals on the Sabbath, again showing that the old order must
be transcended by trust in a new cause. In the face of the loss of the

old order, Jesus returns to the heart of the Old Testament in order to give to the disciples a cause greater than legal regulations: love God and neighbor.

• Jesus accepts women, the poor (who have not fulfilled religious requirements), and public sinners into his fellowship. His invitation is extended to people who have been excluded, who have a personal sense of loss.

• In saying, "Whoever would save his life will lose it [Mark 8:35]," Jesus challenges those who claim to find ultimate fulfillment in material things, in living only for themselves, and in trying to protect themselves as a means to health. For some, this message may have pierced their false security; they may have realized that their claims were indeed misplaced. For those who had already experienced the futility of saving themselves through such action, Jesus' saying comes as a call to redirect their trust and loyalty: "Whoever loses life for my sake and the gospel's will save it [Mark 8:35]."

• A final example, is Mark 10:23ff. This passage is not simply a commentary on the rich young man who could not give up his possessions (his claims to power and status), but on all who seek to lay claim to God's Rule by human power, wisdom, or moral perfection. Jesus resists the conventional expectations that the Holy One can be bargained with, controlled, or possessed by human claims. The disciples are so much at a loss that they exclaim: "Then who can be saved?" The description of this encounter is filled with great emotion, suggesting that it was remembered as a powerful crisis in the disciples' relation to Jesus. Jesus responds with an affirmation of grace, but the grace of the God who shatters all human idols: "With men it is impossible, but not with God; for all things are possible with God."

In all of these examples, we see that Jesus' proclamation of the Rule of God creates a crisis, which allows some people to turn. The act of turning is a process of reorientation. The old values are seen in a new perspective. Some things are set aside (idols are demolished), other things lose their power over us (we are liberated from them), and still others are placed in a new context (they are revalued). These forms of reorientation find ample illustration in our lives. Our world of concern is expanded and made more inclusive. The center of value is no longer the self, the family, the race, or the nation, but the God who creates all things and cares for all with a gracious Rule (God causes the rain to fall upon the evil as well as the good!). The divine will is beyond our comprehension yet is trustworthy when we experience it in the manifestations of personal faithfulness.

The Gift of Healing and the Integrity of the Self

Basic to our conception of turning to God is the experience of the reorientation of the person, as we see ourselves in a new light in the presence of God. Niebuhr argued that the encounter with the one God required a transformation of all things and relations. He went on to suggest that the discovery of the one personal and faithful Self bears directly upon our ability to bring unity to our own lives. We need to bear in mind the essential connection between the English words *holy, whole,* and *heal* (also *hale,* as in "hale and hearty," and *health*); all are derived from the same root. While we can speculate on the reasons that northern European languages made this connection, from a biblical perspective it makes good theology. Sacred power (holiness) reveals itself as healing power; to be holy is to be whole; to possess integrity (to be whole) is the gift of God's healing to us.

Consider the language connections in relation to the way our lives are parceled out in multiple acts of trust and loyalty. We are defined by so many roles and causes (son/daughter, husband/wife, father/mother, sister/brother, member of groups, an employee under authority as well as having authority, citizen, neighbor) that we can well ask, Who am I? The tensions between the commitments inherent in each role or cause lead to boundaries, often created to resolve the tensions. We separate the parts of our lives with different rules, expectations, and values. Work and family, career and play, personal life and business life, or politics and religion—all become different realms of our being. We separate them from one another so that we can legitimate the differences between them and not be bothered by the contradictions. But the long-term effect of these tensions on the person is the separation of selfhood into parts. Where is the one person with a sense that his or her life has a fundamental unity?

If we approach this problem of the divided self with the assumption that the world outside the self is also divided, we rule out any possibility of finding coherence or integration outside of us; then there is even less possibility of integration inside the self. If, for example, the world allows for no connections between the values essential to work in the world and those essential to family life, the distinction becomes a great gulf; we have two unreconciled aspects of our life. A person who adopts a competitive and impersonal corporate code of conduct is soon at odds with traditional family values, such as sharing, honesty, and self-sacrifice. Will the person accept living in two worlds? Doing so could lead to disastrous consequences.

There is one response other than acceptance of the divisions imposed by a divided world, and that is defiance. It is possible for the self to rebel against an inhospitable world in order to create in one life the unity and coherence sought by the self. But even such acts of protest contain a sense of disunity, since a person must live over against that of which he or she is still a part, at least on the level of physical existence if not on the level of the spirit.

In going to the heart of the matter, Niebuhr saw that if God is not the unity of power and goodness—or, we might say, the unity of holy power and healing goodness—then human beings will at the least be dualists. We will have a regard for life-giving power and seek out goodness to enhance our life. But we will avoid death-giving power and oppose what harms our life. If the power that created us, from which we draw daily bread and which forces us to expend ourselves to survive, is not good, then we will invariably respect such power but not love it. Will we not have at least two gods: the one ruling us in our drive for survival and the other attracting us in our need to find meaning and love?

Our mixed reactions to life and death illustrate the tendency toward duality. We want to embrace life and love it to the fullest, but that very life contains the power of our aging and death. The tension within us regarding life and death prompts us to look for a duality outside us: The same One cannot give us newborns and corpses. If we cannot accept our life and death from God, how can we believe in one God?

A variety of divided loves and loyalties points to the same problem. Whether we are torn by the love of two people, caught between spouse and parents, work or family, we experience radically opposing claims upon us. If these tensions are never resolved, we will live a double life, always containing in ourselves two different loves or, even worse, love and hate.

If in a moment of honest introspection we are able to acknowledge the way our lives are divided, or the way that we are at war with ourselves, then we open ourselves to the healing of God's gift. This becomes a cross event. Turning to God is the opportunity to place our ultimate trust and loyalty in the God who is, above all, an integral part of our lives, who places us into a community of grace and wholeness and who unites our disparate selves. The reconciliation that Christ gives to us points in many directions and rightly so: to God, to our neighbor, to the Earth, and to ourselves. Anything less would be a continuation of the fractured state of affairs. The gift of integrity, or wholeness, on the personal level relates directly to our reunion with the Source of all that is and to our reintegration into the human community.

Turning as a Continuous Process

The final point in our discussion of faith in God as the decisive turning relates to its continuing state. Given the multiplicity of the value centers in the world and of our forms of faith, the tension between faith in God and other claims shall continue throughout our lives. Life is a continuous process of assessing our trust and loyalty in light of the great commandment to love God and neighbor. The process of reorientation is continuous. We must avoid the naive confidence that suggests that a turning at a certain point in time shall suffice for a lifetime. We must avoid this, not only because of our tendency to claim too much, but just because we are alive. Neither God nor the self are building blocks put in place on a foundation in one's past. Faith is a present relation to the living God by persons who are continually changing and experiencing new needs, threats, tensions, and dreams. It is in such circumstances that our trust and loyalty live, are challenged, grow, and turn again and again to God. By recognizing constant change we do not say there is no continuity or stability to being Christian. Indeed, we struggle in these continuing crises in the sure knowledge that we have been named by God and that God's goodness toward us is everlasting. In this sense, our turning is discovered as a re-turning to that One who loved us from the beginning.

Summary

By analyzing the work of H. Richard Niebuhr, we have sought to expand our view of faith to include the following: (1) Faith is an expression of our *trust and loyalty* in a world of *multiple centers of value and claims*. (2) We are continually faced with the *conflict* of claims, which *collide* or produce a sense of *loss*. (3) Faith in God is a *continual process of turning* to the One who shatters all false claims and draws us into a new world where all people, relations, and things are reassessed in light of the God who is the source of all that is and who has created all things.

Issues for Reflection and Discussion

1. How do you react to Niebuhr's suggestion that faith often finds expression in pluralism or "social" faith? What forms of social faith do you see today?

2. Niebuhr believed that faith in God is such an unsettling experience that he could only call it radical monotheism. Do you understand God in these terms? What is your reaction to the idea that faith in God requires the loss of old claims and a commitment to a new cause? What is the new cause?

3. Do the ideas and concepts of Niebuhr's approach (crisis, turning, collision, loss, reorientation) help you understand your life, your family, or larger social issues?

Chapter 4

A Model of Conversion

We have been forging a set of concepts in order to understand the process of becoming Christian. These are faith as trust and loyalty; the conflict of faith; and faith's main claims, crises, turnings, and reorientations. In this chapter we shall organize the concepts into a model of conversion. Our goal is a greater understanding of faith and self, which frees us to think and act in ways consistent with the mind of Christ.

Introducing the Model

Christian history is filled with models of becoming and being a Christian. Following the practice of Jesus, the apostles preached the good news. As we have already noted, Acts 2:37 reports that such preaching had success in prompting the listeners to ask, What shall we do? This model continues to this day in evangelical preaching in all branches of the church. But there are other models of conversion present in the New Testament. Acts of healing, works of service, the inclusion of people into a caring and disciplined community, prophecy, sacramental worship, religious music and art, and teaching have all given us models for a turning to God. In modern Protestantism discussions of conversion have focused on the debate about whether conversion is best described as a crisis event or as long-term spiritual nurturance and growth. Conservative revivalism has been the well-known champion of the dramatic decision, whereas ecumenical Protestantism has leaned toward the nurture of the individual through preaching, sacrament, education, and counseling in order to incorporate him or her into the community. In recent years the many socio-psychological theories of human development have provided new conceptual frameworks for understanding both crisis and nurture/ growth experiences.

The model developed here defines conversion as a *process of receiving a new identity and status as a gift from God.* Let us relate this definition to the vocabulary we have already developed.

First, conversion is a process of turning from one state to another. In previous chapters we have argued that the turning is precipitated by a crisis. Here we qualify that in this sense. The turning usually occurs because of a decisive development or event beyond the control of the person. The key is not that it is a short-term, dramatic incident but that it presents the self with a critical change. This change is a crisis in the way previously defined: an unveiling of conflict or loss and the occasion for turning. Therefore, although we can continue to see dramatic events as one form of crisis, changes or events in the life cycle can also be decisive. For example, the transitions from childhood to adolescence or from adolescence to adulthood have all the elements of crisis, though incorporated into a long-term process. These times of transition include a new awareness of what it means to be a person, the loss of a former state, new power and freedom, and the occasion for decisions that will determine the future. Thus, the model is open to gradual processes as well as to the dramatic incident in the life of the individual or society. In all cases something happens that literally pushes the self out of one state, forcing a decision about turning to a new state or retreating to a previous one.

Second, the model speaks of turning from one state of being or self-consciousness to another. By self-consciousness we refer to the way the self defines its identity and perceives the world. Self-consciousness is not formed in isolation from the world but represents the complex interaction of the self in the world and the world upon the self. As the expression of our identity and relation to the world, self-consciousness motivates and controls our action. For example, an inferiority complex represents the way a person defines him- or herself but is also the way the person perceives the world valuing him or her. It is never clear whether the complex arose from something within the person or is a response to treatment by the world. We even speak of "self-fulfilling" behavior, which demonstrates a prior judgment about the person. What is clear, however, is that the inferiority complex becomes a controlling form of self-consciousness, thereby determining what the person will or will not do.

Paul encounters in the Corinthians a self-consciousness based on worldly wisdom. Their identity and status are based on claims to wisdom that bestow upon them maturity and freedom. They perceive the world through these claims, and their actions proceed out of such self-consciousness. In a world where it is important to be wise, they are boastful about their knowledge. In a world that values individual fulfillment, they take pride in acting as they please. That they disrupt the community is of no consequence to them, because the world values the strong individual who succeeds in self-expression. Concern for the common good and self-sacrifice for one's neighbor are low priorities. Their actions are determined as much by their perception of what the world values as by what they value. They affirm worldly wisdom and are prisoners of it.

Third, the model presents three forms of self-consciousness, which are broad images of selfhood. Described below, these images are autonomous life, moral life, and Christian self-consciousness. The images do not represent people, historical periods, or even stages of human development. Perhaps the best way to understand them is as moments in human life. The self can be quite different in different moments. It can undergo change, develop, and consciously alter itself. A moment can capture a person's identity and perception of the world.

But if we speak of three moments in our lives, do they have any continuity? Here we need to recognize that particular moments become the forces that shape our memory, our minds, and our hearts. In some moments we decide for or against one thing, or we are shaped by something. The word *decide* comes from Latin roots that mean "to cut off." When we decide for something, we also cut ourselves off from something else. For example, to decide to marry someone means to set aside romantic relations with other people (a concept American culture finds hard to grasp!). Many married people recall the moment they decided to marry their spouse and continue to see the spouse and their whole life through that one moment. Moments are decisive in shaping the person. We might even say that a person consists of a history of decisive moments, which weave a pattern of personal identity. Thus we consider it quite appropriate for a person to tell us who he or she is by telling us of these decisive moments. It is in this sense that the three forms of self-consciousness are moments.

This decisive-moments approach allows us to avoid thinking of the three forms of self-consciousness as stages, wherein a person would begin with the first and move to the second then the third. To be sure, many people may find such a sequence in their life. But others do not and are confused at the thought that becoming Christian means fitting their life into a preestablished formula.

The concept of decisive life moments allows us to understand all sorts of journeys to becoming Christian. Moreover, it gives us a chance to examine the most complex phenomenon: the continual struggle of Christians with their old forms of life while being Christian. Christians have colorful words to describe their spiritual lives: backsliding, losing the Spirit, feeling spiritually lukewarm, and wandering away. These experiences cannot be understood by a linear, step-by-step process. The fact is, as Paul confesses, we may have more than one moment determining our self-consciousness. Such a process will produce endless tension and paradox in our description of being Christian.

Three Moments in Life

In this section we define the three types of self-consciousness. The crucial issues underlying them are (a) their basis for identity and worth and (b) the type of action that is necessitated or allowed by each state of being.

Autonomous Life

The first form of self-consciousness is *autonomous* self-consciousness. The word literally means self-legislating, or "a law unto oneself." In autonomous life, the individual is perceived as the primary agent, the ultimate determiner of his or her own destiny. The autonomous person assumes self-determination and seeks the goal of self-sufficiency.

There are many forces that push us toward autonomous consciousness. In the first place, as creative, spiritual beings, we exist by means of free action. No matter how strong our group consciousness, we become human by means of a process of individualization. At some point it dawns on each of us that we are a distinct self, who must take responsibility for ourself and affirm ourself through our own actions. This realization is often precipitated by harsh circumstances. Sometimes the discovery that no one else will provide for us forces us to be self-reliant. Some people see autonomous life as the dominant image in American culture. In a nation of colonists, immigrants, pioneers, former slaves, and homsteaders, the push toward autonomous life is both explicit and implicit, written large in popular culture and quietly planted in our souls. The ideals of individual happiness and success reenforce the conviction that identity and worth depend upon individual achievement. Even the seemingly pious verse "God has no hands but our hands" implies that we are the ultimate determiners of life.

There are two major activities of autonomous life. First, the self is taken as *the end,* which is to be created, developed, and perfected. The self is thereby committed to constant activity, to self-assertion. Work, wealth, knowledge, possessions, family, and friends are all part of a world created by the self that is seeking identity and worth.

The drive to self-assertion is filled with paradox. It is an absolutely essential and necessary expression of free creatures. We express our very selves through the work of our minds and hands. To deny free action restricts our participation in the world; but just as important, it denies us our very humanity, since we discover who we are through the actions of our minds and hands.

The drive for self-assertion is, however, easily abused and corrupted. Consider the ways our anxieties and fears channel our actions: Will I have enough money to provide for my family or my retirement? How can I find social acceptance? Will I be able to meet the new demands of my work in a rapidly changing and complex world? Abuse of the drive also occurs through the pressures of the world about us. The ideals of success, wealth, conspicuous consumption, youthful strength and beauty all send a clear message: "Work harder, achieve more, become more attractive; but remember, yesterday's success and achievements will not suffice for tomorrow." Caught between our own fears of failure and powerlessness and the unrelenting demands of the world, the autonomous self works and works, believing that what it does is what it is.

The second form of activity of the autonomous self is defensiveness: the self is viewed as *an object of value to be protected.* If what we create is linked to our identity and worth, then the self has a personal stake in defending its activity. If our action is devalued, then the self also loses value. Consider these personal and emotionally charged words of normal experience: to be wrong, to be disgraced, to appear ignorant, to be put down, to lose social status, to be excluded. The list goes on: to lose one's job, to be passed over in a selection process, to be criticized, to be omitted from a guest list, to lose the game, to come in last, to be seriously ill. All these experiences embody the pain of the ultimate loss, death itself. In a world where everything depends on being active, right, smart, attractive, or powerful, any criticism is a major threat.

Defensiveness employs a wide range of strategies. Denial is the first line of defense. Denial is followed by new attempts to justify our action or, still worse, by attacks on those who dare criticize. Such defensiveness is destructive for more than the obvious reasons. It prevents us from seeing reality as it is—which prevention is what it means to be dishonest. Furthermore, it creates new problems in its aggressive attack on one's opponent. In many cases, the secondary argument becomes worse than the original problem. For example, in the home the problem may not be the burnt toast but the quarrel over who is responsible for it. Or, in the world of national politics, it was not the burglary that produced the disaster of Watergate but the attempt to cover it up! The price we pay for defensiveness is the inability to deal creatively and effectively with the original problem. Why are we willing to hurt ourselves and other people in this manner? Is it not our fear of failure and loss, our desire to maintain power and status in a very demanding and unmerciful world?

The autonomous life, then, seeks to create meaning and value for the self through self-assertion and defensive behavior. The two forms of behavior reenforce one another. They place the self or the group in a constant state of activity, since there can be no rest from the chase, from defensiveness. They also make the person or group a threat to others. Autonomous life defines the center of value in limited terms: one's person, one's family, one's corporation, one's class, one's nation. Autonomous life is, to use Niebuhr's term, inherently henotheistic. Other people or groups are perceived as competitors in a field of action where only some can win and most must lose. Such devaluation of some people is required to elevate one person or group to the place of honor and power. Is it any wonder that autonomous life begins to look like our world of competition and individualism, of bitter exchanges about the merits of personal action or political policy! In its negative side it is the world of claims—our world and that of Corinth.

Moral Life

The great adversary of autonomous life is moral self-consciousness. To some degree moral consciousness exists in every person, group, and culture. It is rooted in the impulses of honesty about what is and of a commitment to positive values such as fairness, love, life, and equality. The moral consciousness arises and develops its critical power through the combination of honesty and commitment to values. Moral consciousness is *the recognition that the self or group is in a state of loss and requires a new mind and/or new action.*

Moral life is only possible through a twofold act of courage: (1) To be honest is to open oneself to the reality outside oneself; and (2) to evaluate one's action by means of positive values is to submit oneself to a standard outside oneself. This twofold activity is a threat to autonomy, since it may mean the loss of control. In autonomous life, the self or the group will decide what is true and what are the standards, even if this requires falsifying reality. Thus, moral life requires courage.

While it requires moral courage to admit one is wrong or ignorant, the movement to moral life is not spontaneously generated by moral convictions alone. In a crisis, such as the cross event that creates a sense of loss, in general, we do not choose to step outside of autonomous life. We are pushed out by the crisis. Something happens that overwhelms us or our group: we simply cannot ignore the contradiction between the status quo and new legitimate values that confront us. Moral courage is the ability to respond to such a crisis, to admit in all honesty that change is needed, and to attempt to actualize the values that are absent.

At the heart of moral life is this paradox: Those who are most conscious of life-giving values are beset by the most profound sense of not possessing them. For example, those who have a clear sense of goodness have a greater sense of guilt. Among those who value knowledge are those with increasing awareness that they know less and less. In a similar way, the artistic eye gives a person a greater sense of the distance between beauty and everyday sights. The sense of loss in moral consciousness can be so overwhelming that everything is seen in terms of a fundamental contradiction. The security and comfort of autonomous life collapses. The very symbols of that security now symbolize a lost cause. Conversely, new symbols emerge out of the crisis as representative of a new world. Autonomous and moral life look at the same events. The former sees, at most, isolated problems that do not touch the basic security of the self or society; the latter sees the events as symbolic of a world in crisis.

Let us reflect upon several examples of a change in perspective. First, within the circle of friendship and family, an event can occur that forces us to see everything in a new light. Physical or psychological abuse, a dishonest or cruel remark, a break in trust—any one of these can precipitate a crisis, causing us to flee from relationships that are oppressive or crippling.

Second, for many years as a sign of prosperity, stock certificates portrayed industrial plants with smoke pouring out of chimneys. Now such a symbol means a disregard for the environment and human life.

Third, the death of Martin Luther King, Jr., in 1968 came as a cross event. Until then we may have recognized that there were some problems in the United States but considered them to be isolated problems. Most Americans could still affirm with pride that as a nation we possessed a just and fair social order. But King's death overwhelmed us; it pushed us out of the security of American autonomous life into a frightening realization that something was wrong. How ironic that King's death came shortly before Holy Week. Many Christians enter Holy Week and experience the official Good Friday with little sense of terror or grief; now for the first time many of us discovered what being in the wrong before a cross event really meant. As with so many events in that period, the symbols of law and order became symbols of the mechanisms of segregation and abuse of power.

Fourth, some of us who concluded that the Viet Nam War was unjustifiable can usually point to some event that pushed us out of the security of the official national policy. Perhaps it was the endless rationalizations regarding casualty counts or the word games (e.g., offensive military actions were called "protective reaction strikes"). Many remembered the national news showing a South Vietnamese officer executing a prisoner. That picture became symbolic of the crisis. Something was wrong; there was a gap between reality and ideals.

Personal moral consciousness produces two forms of activity: criticism and action. When they are governed by positive values, they can result in creative reform. Criticism represents the power of analytic reason in the service of moral standards. Moral life raises legitimate values—often the very ones the culture celebrates in monuments and public buildings—and applies them to the situation. Criticism in the form of evaluation, review, protest, or angry outrage all stem from the desire to be honest. But the degree of emotion expresses the degree to which personal identity and worth are threatened by the crisis. When we experience the loss of our claims, we ask the revolutionary question, What shall I do? Our desire is to reclaim or recreate our value through action. Thus, reform movements for the protection of children, for peace, for the environment, for schools, or for the care of the aged come into being. A felt need is analyzed as a problem, and a commitment is made to do something about it.

But a break in the connection between criticism and values often leads to counterproductive results. The overly critical person may display a sense of superiority and freedom. He or she is able to judge all things and appear above all that is average or flawed. But like adolescents who often fail to place criticism in the context of concern and helpfulness, such people are hard to live with. Their self-righteousness separates them from other mortals, and they fail to assist others in improving the situation. Failure is inherent in self-righteousness because of the risk in claiming that we can improve anything. What if we fail? Are we then not destroyed by the critical powers that we have wielded with such force?

Before leaving the discussion of moral consciousness, we should note three additional forms of behavior that reflect, in very different ways, a distortion of moral passion: despair, rage, and terrorism. Despair arises when one realizes that nothing can be done to change the situation for the good. The person's hopelessness, however, still reflects the desire for those values that could redeem the situation. In a different way, rage also points to moral values, though in a disruptive and violent way. The moral life generates tremendous passion against a wrong, a passion expressed in rage. Even though rage is a distortion, it is the positive commitment to a value that is at its heart. For example, student protests in the 1960s reflected the angry reaction against social evils that could not be accepted or overcome by nonviolent means. The most extreme form of the moral passion for justice is the fanticism of terrorism. Terrorists are so convinced that they are the victims of evil and that righteousness is on their side, that they feel justified in taking violent action. The fact that such action denies the value they seek or perpetuates new evils on innocent people is lost in the face of their rage and moral righteousness.

It needs to be clear that moral life assumes that the self is capable of the change and creativity required to overcome the loss discovered in the crisis. In this *it shares the same fundamental assumption of autonomous life, namely, that the self creates its own identity and worth.* The contradictions discovered in moral courage (moral wrong, lack of knowledge, powerlessness) can, will, and should be resolved through new action of the self or the group. Moral life differs from autonomous life in its conviction that it will create a new and higher order. The danger of moral life is, therefore, the possibility that the self or the group cannot redeem the situation. In such a situation moral life faces the crisis of its own failure. Moral courage must then face the fact that the self or the group is permanently estranged from the very values necessary for its existence. At this point the sense of loss is complete. What started with a sense of loss ends in a new and more personal sense of loss, the inability to create the new order.

Christian Self-Consciousness

The sense of loss found in moral life creates an intolerable situation. The person may move back to some form of autonomous life, remain in a state of moral honesty seeking renewal, or find a new mode of existence. Consider the young Martin Luther, bordering on a breakdown. He was obsessed with the idea of moral goodness in the face of a righteous God. The more he followed the advice of his teachers and counselors, the more stressed he became. The churchly status quo of the time was in effect an autonomous consciousness: One accepted the claims of the church and did what one could; moral and religious action became the basis for identity before God. Applying moral honesty to such an approach, Luther found it incomprehensible that a person's standing before God could depend on the person's action. He could find no peace until he broke with the claims of an autonomous church, as well as with the moral claim that he could justify himself before God. Luther's so-called revolution was the rediscovery of Paul's message that salvation is a gift received in trust of the heart.

Christian consciousness arises out of the crisis precipitated by either the autonomous or the moral life. In the face of loss and radical honesty about such loss, a person has a new self-consciousness born in *the acknowledgement that identity and worth are gifts of God.* Two life-giving consequences proceed from this conversion.

The end of self-sufficiency. Let us begin here by recalling Paul's message to the Corinthians. Paul affirmed that saving knowledge and power are not in us or our achievement but are things we receive. His theology of the cross was intended to bring to an end the pervasive human ideal that we possess the power and knowledge to control our destiny. The sovereign God judges such pride, but, more important, enters the world in the form of a servant to draw us to life and light.

This is the primary meaning of grace: life is a gift; we do not create our identity and world.

It is only when we grasp the full meaning of grace as the basis for a new self-consciousness that we understand the many references to freedom, joy, and gratitude in Christian speech. Grace means the liberation from the obsessive drive *to do something worthy* in the endless task of creating status. The burden of such self-sufficiency and assertiveness is removed, in fact, it now appears somewhat comic! Moreover, grace means the liberation from *defensiveness*. Since our worth and identity are now guaranteed by God, nothing can change that, whether it be the imperfections of our own action or the claims of others.

For many people liberation from self-criticism may be more significant than the freedom from the criticism of others. Both autonomous and moral life can be devastating in their self-criticism. The new Christian freedom does not mean a disregard for standards, that nothing matters. In one sense, things are taken more seriously because our whole life is placed before God. Christian freedom is the knowledge of who we are, what we have done, what we can and cannot do in the presence of a gracious God. If God is gracious and supportive of us, then for the first time we can be gracious to ourselves.

It is the introduction of grace, as a new reality freely given by God, that is a radical change from both autonomous life and moral life. The movement beyond moral life is especially significant because morality can be so demanding. It is an ever-present imperative to do the good, but it offers little comfort when we fail. By contrast, love always goes beyond the demands of the law and creates a new reality. Christian being arises when we discover that a power other than our own has placed us in a new reality where we are claimed by a gracious love. It is no accident that those who receive this new being may discover the true meaning of Sabbath rest (that is, the end of our frantic self-assertion and defensiveness). Without fear or shame we are free to be in the presence of God and, therefore, in the presence of ourself and other people.

The beginning of new life. To receive a new identity and worth in the presence of God is also to be renewed. The crisis that pushed us to turn was both the awareness of loss and a desire for the new. Becoming Christian is the awareness that we are called to participate in a new community where the spirit of God gives life and makes possible the renewal we seek. Jesus makes this clear in his teaching about the rule of God: The new age is at hand; therefore, those who hear this news and trust in the gracious power of God are enabled to act in new ways—faithfully, hopefully, and lovingly. The key here is the new reality, or context. In autonomous life one is competing with others and on one's own. Love, humility, and sharing make no sense in theory or practice. Christian conversion is the recognition of the new reality that allows us to act in new ways. We can accept others because we are accepted; we can be humble because our status is secure and not a work of self. We can share in the confidence that God will provide for all of us. Reality is, in effect, re-created by God in Christ. We are now in Christ, or have the mind of Christ. We live, not for ourselves, but for God and one another.

Here again Christian consciousness goes beyond moral life but not in the sense of personal perfection. (Christians are not superior to nonreligious morally serious persons.) It refers to the movement beyond criticism. Criticism can be a way of life that prevents one from trying anything, lest he or she fail. The Christian willingness to risk efforts toward renewal lies in the confidence that such efforts are not a new claim to self-justification. Nor are such efforts based on our power and wisdom, but on the power and wisdom of Christ. Christians dare speak of a new holiness (that is, healing and wholeness), not because it is our creation, but because it is the gift of God. We are commanded to hope and pray for new life, because it is already in our midst in the Spirit of Christ and is promised to us for the future.

Is it any wonder that the gift, the promise of God, has inspired countless reform movements in the history of the church? Those who live in the new freedom of Christ are empowered to act in new ways. This action is always taken in the face of great risk, not simply in the light of their critics, but also from their own fear of inadequacy in contrast to the perfect love and justice of God. In the ideal, Christians should deal with this tension through constant self-criticism by the Word of God. Whatever we propose or achieve must be examined and recognized as less than the final will of God. That we Christians have not always kept to the ideal but made our achievements the basis for lofty claims, points to one reason that conversion is a life-long process.

Summary

We started with the assumption that human beings are creatures of trust and loyalty, involved in claims and conflict of claims. Our model of conversion describes human life as a continual process of interaction among three decisive moments (the autonomous, moral, and Christian life), each having the power to determine our minds and hearts. The analysis of autonomous and moral consciousness attempts to open up for inspection all aspects of our life, whether prior to or alongside of our Christian being. The model assumes that the two moments are, in varying degrees, a part of our life and that through the experience of crisis we are pushed into a time of turning toward Christian consciousness.

Tension Between Autonomous and Christian Life

The model makes clear the inevitable and fundamental tension between the autonomous and the Christian life. Both affirm the possibility of meaning and value, but in opposite ways. Trust and loyalty are directed either toward the self and group or toward God. The former results in exclusive claims, which tend toward idolatry. Becoming Christian always requires the forsaking of idols and a reassessment of all our centers of value.

The tension is not restricted, however, to a once-for-all disowning of worldly claims. As Christian history and our own experience reveal, Christian life is always in danger of being adapted to pluralistic or henotheistic faiths. We adapt or accommodate Christian faith to our many centers of value. The faith in the universal God becomes restricted to particular interests in one time and place. God is no longer the Creator of all people and things, but our God and only our God. Jesus' teachings are domesticated, so that he no longer calls us to take up God's cause but blesses whatever causes we propose. God is then defined, perhaps, as male, white, Western, and the advocate of our industry and technology. (In its opposite ideological form, God is defined as nonwhite, of the Third World, and the advocate of revolution.) In this way we are protected from experiencing any crisis, even though such accommodation is oppressive.

In the face of the continual tendency to identify the gift with our claims, we need to keep before us the tension between Christian life and autonomous life. There are gifts of the Spirit that help us: Regular reading of scripture can be a crisis-engendering act; Sabbath worship includes penitential prayer and honest preaching; and the church year provides endless festivals that break into our accommodation with the world.

There is also a continuing tension between the Christian and the moral consciousness that is somewhat paradoxical. On the one hand, Christians can and should be sympathetic to all acts of moral courage, which call us to see reality in honest ways. On the other hand, Christian life must break with moral life in the confession that the renewal of ourselves and the world is a gift of grace. This act of faith and hope allows us to move beyond criticism to acts of reconciliation and healing. Christian life does not make a superior claim to righteousness but points to the gift of righteousness given to all creation.

The next chapter provides opportunity to use the model of conversion in a variety of contexts. You may wish to review it immediately as a simple means of personally relating to the model.

Issues for Reflection and Discussion

1. Consider the concept of "the moment" as defined in this chapter. What are the decisive moments in your life? in the life of your family? How have they shaped your thought and action?
2. Consider the basic ideas involved in the autonomous and the moral consciousness. Do you see either as an image of selfhood in any moments in your life? in the life of your family or friends? in our society? in the church?
3. What are the strengths and weaknesses of autonomous and moral consciousness? Could we live without these moments? Can we live with them?
4. How do you react to the definition of Christian consciousness? Is it your view or experience of Christian faith?

Chapter 5

Surveying the Contours
And Boundaries of
Our Hearts

If chapter 4 presents the model of conversion in theory, this chapter provides a practical guide for using it. The model has value only as a means for understanding the many forces at work in the process of becoming and being Christian. To begin, we review the broad outline of the model. Let us keep in mind four points. First, three forms of self-consciousness (autonomous, moral, and Christian) may be seen as moments in a person's life. One of the three may become dominant over time. Second, movement between the three forms is usually caused by a crisis, which pushes the self out and offers the possibility of turning to the gift of Christ. Third, movement is possible in any direction. Some will find that their life tells the story of a constant movement toward God's gift, from autonomous, to moral, to Christian life. Others will find that they began as Christians and were pushed out of a naive belief system, or simply lost it, and have now returned after livng in moments of autonomous and moral life. Each person may tell a different story of turning. Finally, movement is continuous. Christian being is always at risk of compromise and in need of renewal.

Three Applications

As an introduction into the application of the model to concrete situations, several cases are offered as illustrations. The cases point to the frequency of occurrence of claiming, crisis, cross event, and reorientation in human experience. After examining the way the categories have been used to interpret these cases, this chapter presents an exercise through which the reader may scrutinize personal life experience with the model in mind.

Mark 10: Claims, Collision, Loss, Turning, Trust

The tenth chapter of Mark presents a dazzling mix of stories that present alternating positions between conflict, bitter disappointment, and trust in God. The chapter begins with a tense confrontation between Jesus and the Pharisees over the interpretation of the law regarding divorce. Jesus will not accept the premise that life in God's realm, including married life, is a bargain or contract based on legalities. He reaffirms an intention of God for persons to seek an indissoluble union.

This scene is followed by the surprising insistence by Jesus that the children brought to him (possibly for blessing) be allowed to be part of the gathering. Children are a key to the realm of God because of their dependence and utter trust in their parents. They are without status or power. The critique of all our claims—whether autonomous or moral—to make ourselves acceptable to God could not be imaged more clearly. In this story, following upon that of Jesus' confrontation with the legalists, Mark gives us a clue to the life of faith. One must accept the rule of God as a gift in utter trust.

Jesus then meets the rich man who asks what is required for salvation. We are somewhat uneasy in our approach to this story, because we fear it is directed against our possessions and wealth. But, in fact, the story is more about claims than wealth per se. This man has done everything and has everything in order—or so it seems— except for one thing. He is so attached to his riches that he cannot give them up, even for his very salvation.

Wealth is one of the primary ways we claim identity and worth. It suggests a wide range of social relations involving superiority, power, and authority. The rich man wants to enter God's realm with all of these relations in tact, no matter how oppressive or illusory. Jesus' request that he give up his wealth asks him to give up his autonomy. It breaks the man's heart, because he cannot do it. Here is a collision between two definitions of life: It is created by our success or it is a gift. The man cannot and will not lose his worldly status.

The departure of the man who loved his possessions more than

God gives Jesus the opportunity to comment on the danger of riches (10:23). As we have noted, Mark's emotional description of this encounter suggests that it was remembered as a powerful crisis in the disciples' relation to Jesus. they were "amazed" and "exceedingly astonished" (vv. 24–26) at Jesus' rejection of the man and confront him with their bewilderment: "Then who can be saved?" What worldly assumptions go into this question? Do the disciples assume that wealth and success grant certain access to salvation?

Verse 27 says that Jesus "looked" at them before responding. Can you imagine that look? Was it disappointment or a flash of anger? Perhaps Jesus was pushing them, hoping they would arrive at the point of losing all claims. In this he succeeded, for they appear to be acknowledging that we cannot save ourselves by our claims. No matter how prestigious or righteous we may be, Jesus can now affirm the true and only basis for our trust: the gracious God who makes all things possible, even the salvation of those who have no claims.

Still, after the response of Jesus about the possibilities of God, Peter is confused! "Lo, we have left everything, and followed you [v. 28]." Peter wants a relation to Jesus and God based on compensation for what he has done. Is not all that we do the basis for our standing before God? Was not leaving family a bargain that deserves a reward? Let the rich man weep, since he refused to give up his possessions. But the disciples left work and families and now deserve special status. Again Jesus confronts this misguided claim on God with the reminder that the last shall be first and the first last.

As if this symbol of God's reversal of roles were not enough, Mark next includes a prediction of Jesus' crucifixion and resurrection. For the legalists, the rich man, and the disciples, Mark presents Jesus as the one who puts aside all claims for himself and relies completely upon the will of God. This is a rebuke of Peter's confusion, and it serves as a prelude to the self-serving request of James and John. When asked if they are able to drink from the same cup, they answer with all the false confidence one could possibly imagine. The tension between human self-interest and the will of God, between the way of ruling over people and the way of service, is clear. Since the disciples do not see what it means to turn to God, Mark introduces a blind beggar (vv. 46–52), who sees clearly what it means to trust in God and receive a gift.

All of this is in one chapter in Mark! We have here the repeated collision between our claims and Jesus' affirmation of God's gift. Pharisees, a rich man, Peter, James, and John seem unable to comprehend, because they fear losing their claims. Only children and a blind man receive the gift. From the perspective of worldly wisdom, Jesus appears to affirm riddles about the last and the first, or serving and ruling. They are incomprehensible, unless one opens oneself to the gift and lives in the new reality that God creates. For those who have received new life in the love of God, self-giving love is the true life.

The American Success Syndrome

One of our culture's versions of the autonomous life is the American success syndrome. We can outline it in broad terms to make clear how it embodies claims and values antithetical to Christian faith. At the same time it must be remembered that not everyone who works in America, or even succeeds, believes in the syndrome or conforms to it.

The ideal of success in America embodies the momentous assumptions that we are what we achieve; that life is a great race; that everyone starts at the same place with the same opportunity; that the goal is success, which confers status, material rewards, access to people and places; and, most important, that happiness will follow.

To say this ideal embodies claims regarding identity and worth is an understatement. For some it has become a world view to be affirmed and defended at all costs. Consider the requirements placed upon those who inherit or choose this life. These include:

• Unlimited demands on one's time and energy, irrespective of family or interests.
• A competitive environemnt at one's work and between one's company and other companies (competitors). (This set of relations is often described in the language of sports, although images of war and the jungle are also common.)
• An individualistic outlook, based on the fact that one is competing with coworkers and paid on the basis of individual performance.
• The overriding value of short-term results. Individual achievement is the basis for rewards or punishments (e.g., small salary increase, reassignment to an unimportant role, or being fired). It is not surprising that the culture of success puts a priority on quantity of production and profits. The new form of short-term results is the phenomenon of mergers, acquisitions, and takeovers, wherein all of

the intellectual and financial power of corporate leadership is directed toward making money, not producing better products, enhancing long-term goals, or broadening social benefits. Ivan Boesky is but one example.

• Corporate loyalty taking precedence over all personal or social values. Individuals are expected to tolerate violations of their personal value system (the operative words are "worldly sophistication") and remain silent regarding practices that may be contrary to the law, harmful to the environment, or excessively competitive (the key phrases are "hard-nosed" and "bottom line").

Those who succeed receive the benefits of this culture: salary, status, and access. But we have read about or seen enough people caught up in this culture of success to know that not everything is as bright as it appears. What happens to human beings when their identity is defined entirely by their job or, even more important, their level of success? They have staked their life on a claim that is inherently contradictory as well as fragile. Narrative reports on people who have lost their jobs reveal the sense of personal loss and emptiness. Being shunned by friends and former associates reenforces their sense of having become a nonperson in a world where only achievement counts.

The race to success has dangerous effects upon the health of people. Studies abound regarding the negative consequences on physical and emotional health. The loss of contact with family and friends produces a tremendous personal and social cost. It is difficult to live in two worlds, the world of work and the world of family, religion, and personal life. Shall we try to reconstruct the world of work according to the values of our private lives? Some would give that little chance. But what if we begin to impose the values of work on our personal lives? Are children products, assets, or employees? Shall the family compete for attention or love, distributed according to achievements? Should we invest time with our spouse according to what we can get in return? These are all questions that we can pose for discussion, but unfortunately they have been actualized in far too many situations. Divorce, ulcers, heart attacks, alcoholism, and emotional breakdowns are part of the culture of success. The record shows that many people pay a high price to be part of this culture, especially since its lauded goal is to make us happy.

There are also social consequences of the success syndrome that must be mentioned. Does the culture of success deliver what it promises? Not everyone succeeds; in fact, many are disabled or discarded by the process that recognizes only short-term profits. Mergers, acquisitions and takeovers make great news for those who may benefit, but what of those adversely affected by these broad shifts in plant locations and investments? Someone pays the price for such dislocation.

One is tempted to say that people are happy to the extent that they have not accepted the success syndrome or allowed it to control their lives. In its very nature it is idolatrous—claiming to give people identity and worth based on financial success and material posses-sions. It is inevitably divisive—pitting people against one another and forcing them to choose between success and the other values they know are life-giving.

The future of this culture of success contains some ironic dimen-sions. At a time when men have received heavy criticism for creating the syndrome and allowing themselves to be victimized by it, more and more women are entering the corporate world. One theory is that women, many of whom have only watched the destructive con-sequences of the success syndrome, humanize the world of work. But the other possibility is that some become part of the culture of success and face all the consequences their male coworkers experience. A second ironic dimension is that while the middle-age generation has become aware of the human cost and outright idolatrous character of the culture of success, many in the younger generation have dedicated themselves with utter abandon to the dream of corporate success. The unsettling thing is that many are succeeding. They report high starting salaries, imminent promotions, and a BMW in the driveway. What one generation waited several decades for is immediately present for another. But this single-mindedness regarding success has meant the subordination of other aspects of life. The younger generation has been marked by such radical individualism that friendship, marriage, and children are often seen as threats to their identity. The idealism of youth is subordinated to concerns for individual security and success.

Waging War on the Earth

In our century the pollution of the Earth has become one of the most terrifying forms of violence. It demonstrates Niebuhr's concept of henotheism in a tragic way. One part of a whole excludes another part and declares it has no value. Humanity ignores its relation to the Earth and violates the Earth as if it were an enemy rather than our home. This devastation has been repeated many times. We see it in the pollution of rivers and lakes, the lowering of the water tables, dumping of toxic waste at Love Canal, the use of Agent Orange in Viet Nam and its devastation of our veterans, the pollution of Lake Superior by the mining industry, the falling of acid rain in the Northeast, and generation of multiple types of air pollution.

The crisis is so commonplace that we can describe a basic pattern that illustrates the conflict of claims present in this warfare. First is an initial discovery of human illness or desecration of the earth. Then an investigation of the problem follows, with the government indicating it has no knowledge of the problem and industries denying that they are in any way connected with it. A sequence of claims and counterclaims develops, leading to the polarization of communities. The resulting debates usually demonstrate considerable shock, defensiveness, and fear. Then people are faced with a sudden and full disclosure that pollution has occurred, that it has caused the problems at hand and those who caused them knew about them all along and denied them, and that the government was either negligent in its duty or chose not to investigate. Such a disclosure precipitates a crisis of immense proportion. It is a cross event, where claims are exposed and people feel a great loss. In the end a final stage of resolution occurs, though the resolution is seldom adequate in terms of compensation or restoration.

This cycle can be analyzed using the categories of claims and crisis. At the outset there is an amazing absence of claims. No one, whether government or industry, knows anything about the problem. In the case of the 1989 Alaskan oil spill, Exxon could not deny its involvement, but the company readily denied negligence regarding the supervision of the crew and the company's preparedness to deal with a problem that many saw as inevitable. It apparently never occurred to the government or the company that ships might collide or run aground.

But environmental controversies soon evoke multiple claims and counterclaims. The dominant mood of those in authority usually tends to be defensive. Authorities cannot admit that the community or industry could be creating a hazard. This defensiveness is quickly picked up by all parts of the community, especially those in the labor force. Environmentalism has been labelled a cause of outsiders and do-gooders; it is a threat to jobs and the value system that has supported the culture. If what is charged is true, then a terrifying crisis would be at hand. What we valued and trusted as life-giving (that is, our way of life or our local industry) would be revealed as the source of death. The vehemence of the resistance attests to the fear that this crisis could contain a cross, the unveiling that something is wrong.

Defensiveness also appears in the final stage of resolution. Even after the problem has been admitted to, with responsibility clearly assigned, the general public is reluctant to insist on harsh punishment or radical changes. Those who brought the problem to light are still seen as causing the problem and may be shunned. They indirectly force other people to ask whether we are all involved in a culture of over-consumption and waste. In effect, they query the claims of our culture: that we are justified in extracting resources from the earth at an extraordinary rate; that we are justified in consuming so much more than Third World nations; and that our policies and life-style are good, although they bring harm to people in general, to our own families, and to the Earth.

The issue of pollution is larger than the problem of roadside litter and preserving national parks. It challenges Western culture. Only moral courage will allow us to overcome our defensiveness that it arouses. The revelation of the actual facts in any major case of pollution inevitably presents a cross event. It unveils the possibility that trust was placed in false claims, that we have been manipulated and used for special interests, that human beings have been hurt and the Earth is in the process of being destroyed.

This revelation leaves people in a state of shock and loss. For families suffering illness or loss of property, it is terrifying to be informed that the damage has been caused by corporate or government policy. That the Earth and human life should be sacrificed for profit or pleasure is the experience of the cross. At the same time, those who defend the status quo as a general act of loyalty also feel a loss. They too are deceived and manipulated. A policy of contempt gave them false information for years, and they were set against their neighbors for the sake of special interests.

Such crises lead ultimately to the issue of reordering our trust. Shall we turn to policies and practices that are more life-giving, or shall we ignore the problems and retreat to a defense of the status quo? The environmental issue requires a more radical shift in our realm of loyalty than we often care to admit. For example, in many controversies, some group appears on the scene taking the side of animals and the Earth. It argues that animals have value and that they must not be destroyed because of short-term human interests. The thought that a species of fish has rights protected by the Constitution strikes most people as either absurd or quaint. The environmentalists are abruptly dismissed or politely thanked for their eccentric opinions. This rejection forces the group to convert its argument from advocating the inherent value of fish (and all other parts of the creation) to a human-centered argument: If the fish do not survive, humanity will not survive. This change in the argument has a major effect. It merits our attention; it receives a serious response and, in many cases, positive action. But consider the meaning of this shift in light of Niebuhr's affirmation of monotheism and the idolatry of exclusive claims. The shift affirms that nothing has value unless it is of value to us! This is the most blatant idolatry and is inherently divisive. It pits us against one another and the Earth itself.

The environmental crisis is really a crisis of our faith. Shall we reorder our loyalties in ways that will be more supportive of all life on this planet? The initial question is, Do every person and all things included in our realm of value require of us respect and loyalty? When we ask that question and explore its many dimensions, then we can begin to place in proper context a variety of other issues: How shall we use the Earth? How may we adapt to it? Should the process of producing anything include the cost of disposal?

As environmental disasters become larger in scope and we become globally more interdependent, environmental questions will probably constitute the greatest challenge to our limited claims. Only the issue of war and peace is of greater urgency. But in a real sense the two coalesce. The issue of the environment is really the issue of peace on the Earth and with the Earth.

Summary and Issues for Reflection

To illustrate how the model of conversion can be used to analyze and interpret the Bible or our common experience, we have examined three cases: Mark 10, as a collection of encounters between Jesus and people; the American success syndrome; and the pollution of the Earth. In all three we found claims, conflict over claims, crises that involve a sense of loss and collision of values, a cross event (i.e., the disappointment and suffering that arise when we discover that trust has been placed in the wrong values or that those in authority do not value humane interests), and the need for reorientation.

Before turning to the reflection exercises that follow, you may want to consider these three cases and conduct your own analysis, with these questions in mind:

1. How does each illustrate the concepts of claiming, crisis, cross event, and reorientation?

2. Why is there such resistance to admitting the need for reorientation?

3. In each case, what is the connection between the claim and the mode of behavior of the persons involved? Can the behavior be changed without changing the claim?

4. Which of the three cases was easiest to understand? If the answer is Mark 10, why was that the case? Why is it easier to apply the concepts to a Bible passage than to contemporary experience?

Using the Language of Crisis and Turning: Reflection Exercises

The remainder of this chapter cites biblical stories and presents situations that may be analyzed with the concepts developed in the earlier chapters and thus integrated into the model of conversion. Bible passages, common experiences, and personal reflection together portray the process of conversion from various perspectives, fleshing out this critically important human and Christian experience.

Old Friends Revisited

The following passages are well-known, and each offers a crucial insight into conversion. One or a few at a time may be selected for study and reflection.

1. Crisis as the presence of God
   a. Psalm 139   The Wonder of God
   b. Luke 1:46–55   The Magnificat
   c. Matthew 6:24–34   Two Masters; Be Not Anxious
   d. Matthew 10:34–39   Reordering Family Relations
   e. Mark 1:16–20; 8:31–38; 10:23–45   Discipleship
2. The Gift is Offered

   a. Luke 15:11–32   The Prodigal Son
   b. Matthew 20:1–16   The Laborers in the Vineyard
3. Life in the Presence of the Gift
   a. Matthew 5:1–12   The Beatitudes
   b. Matthew 7:7–12   Ask, and It Will Be Given You
   c. Matthew 5:21–48   I Say to You

Reading the Times

In this section we have the opportunity to analyze common experiences with vocabulary developed in our model of conversion. It is again appropriate to select one or two areas for reflection, rather than attempt to do all sections.

A conflict of claims. Most congregations have had at least one good debate over the church's relation to moral reform in society. Do the three forms of consciousness help explain why these debates are so complex and intense?

For example, what would be the reaction of autonomous or moral life to these: An issue of race relations in the community? an issue of nuclear disarmament? Do *claims* and *crisis* enter into the debate? Did anybody *turn* to a new position?

The crisis of loss. In many ways we experience loss, which shatters our security and claims. We discover how vulnerable we are and must face all sorts of questions regarding identity, worth, fairness, and meaning. Consider one of these experiences that has been a part of your life from the standpoint of the model.

   1. The loss of a job.
   2. A death of a family member or friend.
   3. Alcoholism and the conceptual framework of A.A.
   4. Any one of the social crises in the past twenty years.

Questions to ask about the situation include: To what extent did the situation become a crisis? Did you see people, relations, and things in a new way? Was there a need to place trust and loyalty in a new center of value? What was the new center? Could you go back to life as it was lived before the crisis?

The Story of Our Lives

Give some thought to your personal history from the standpoint of the model. How would you tell your story? Would it involve moments akin to autonomous, moral, and Christian consciousness? Have there been any crises or turnings?

Use one of the following exercises to reflect upon your life.

1. *The Treasure of Your Heart.*
   a. Defining the Treasure
      What is the most important thing in your life? What do you value the most? What is your greatest achievement?

   b. What Is Its Price?
      How do you feel about the things you answered to in *a*? How do those close to you feel about these things? Do they also value what you value? How does society value these things? Is it important to you that those close to you or society affirm your treasure?

   c. One Among Many Treasures
      Have the things you mentioned in *a* always been what you treasured? What did you value as a teenager, young adult, ten years ago? What caused a change of heart?

   d. Securing Your Treasure
      How did you achieve or secure the things you treasure? What was the consequence of this process? Were there winners and losers?

   e. How Secure Is Your Treasure?
      To keep your treasure, what must you continue to do? What happens if you can't do that anymore? Can you lose your treasure? What happens if it loses its value?

   f. Your Treasure and Your Heart
      Has your treasure been a positive factor for you? How is your health? How are your relations with family, friends, colleagues? Has anyone else benefited from your treasure? Has your treasure allowed you to be responsible to God?

2. *Personal Relations.* Consider your relations with several people close to you (in the family, at work, in church).

    a. What is the basis for your relationship?

    b. What roles are involved?

    c. Are needs of each person met? Do you feel you give or receive more than the other person? Why? How do you deal with this?

    d. How does the relationship deal with problems?

    e. How does the relationship embody the basic ideas of the three moments in the model:
       —self-sufficiency (assertion and defensiveness)
       —honesty and desire for change
       —acceptance and the celebration of grace

3. *In God We Trust.*

    a. Consider the nature of your faith and your relation to God. Perhaps the following questions will assist you in gaining a perspective on your religious journey. Begin with the broad outline H. Richard Niebuhr provides:

       (1) Do you experience life as many centers of value, with God, or the church, as one among many? How do they all connect? How do you deal with the conflicts between the centers?

       (2) Do you have strong commitments directed toward a set of values or a group, such as the family, work, the nation? How do you react to Niebuhr's suggestion that such trust is exclusive because it only gives loyalty to one part? Do you sense in any way that such trust is limited? Does it ever put you in a crisis?

       (3) Do you ever find yourself overwhelmed by a sense that the true God is more than you ever realized? Read Psalm 139. Have there been moments when you relied on God in utter trust? Have there been times when you decided to commit yourself to God's cause?

b. How would you describe your faith as a relation to God?

(1) Is it a bargain that supports your drive for self-sufficiency? If you do something, do you expect God to respond?

(2) Is it a moral challenge that excites you and motivates you to seek a higher standard? Do you ever get worn out? What happens when you fail?

(3) Is it the acceptance of God as sovereign over your life, as the One who judges all things and gives life to all?

c. Have there been crises in your life? What was the sense of loss? To what did you turn?

d. If you see your relation to God drawing on all three types in our model, as represented in *b* above, go further in reflecting upon the way such faith gives shape to life:

(1) How does faith as a bargain shape your identity and relations with other people?

(2) How does faith as a moral challenge affect your self-image and relations with other people?

(3) How does faith as acceptance of the gifts of God determine your identity and relations with other people?

e. If faith is to be directed to the sovereign and gracious God, what reordering and reassessment is needed?

(1) Do your priorities (claims and centers of value) need to be reviewed?

(2) What is your sense of the gifts of God? Do you live in the knowledge of God's acceptance? Are you gracious to yourself?

(3) Have you experienced the freedom of Christ, that is, the release from claims and counterclaims?

(4) Is joy a characteristic of your life? Would your friends know your faith?

(5) Is gratitude a dominant characteristic of your life? Do you thank God for anything? Do you thank people around you for anything?

f. What does trusting in the holy and healing God mean to you?

(1) To what extent is trust in God an occasion for a reuniting of the parts of your life? Do you have a greater sense of wholeness, or integrity, as one who trusts God?

(2) Has trusting God brought you to a new sense of commitment to God's cause? Where do witness, service, and giving enter into your life? Do you see these acts of discipleship as joyful acts of gratitude?

Chapter 6

Living in the Promise

Just what shall we become as Christians? To restate the question in more theocentric terms: What would God have us be? The gift of grace always includes the promise of new life; in fact, the two should never be separated. The gift is the promise, and the promise is given in gracious love. But the gift and the promise have not always been joined. We confess each day that we are nurtured by grace, but we have not always acknowledged the promise of new life. This chapter is the proper conclusion of our discussion on conversion. It is about living in the promise, or reconnecting the gift and the promise.

The Risk of the Promise

Shall We Be Changed?
Marxism challenges people with the saying "The task is not to interpret the world, but to change it!" As a criticism of idle speculation it is helpful. But Christians must take exception to it on two counts: Before we can change the world, we must reinterpret or reconceive the world; before we can change the world, we must be changed.

The first stipulation affirms more than the fact that we need a plan. It affirms that we need a new plan, one that will liberate us from the bondage to what Paul calls worldly wisdom. If there is no movement beyond the drive for self-sufficiency or for reform based on our best interests, then the change will be limited to rearranging things. Is this not why Jesus' initial declaration is so powerful: "The time is fulfilled, and the kingdom of God is at hand; repent, and believe in the gospel [Mark 1:15]."

The second stipulation affirms that we cannot seek to change the world unless we ourselves are changed. This is not the same as saying that first we must become perfect in order to begin to change the social order. Such a view would confine us to inactivity during a very long waiting period. Rather, it affirms that our ability to affect the world is directly related to the change in us. This statement must be interpreted in two ways.

First, it means that we can see ourselves and the world in new ways only if we take on the mind of Christ: "From now on, therefore, we regard no one from a human point of view. . . . Therefore, if any one is in Christ, that one is a new creation [2 Cor. 5:16–17]." We cannot change our lives, our relations, or the structures of the world for the better if we do not embody the new reality. Consider again Jesus' admonition: "So, every sound tree bears good fruit, but the bad tree bears evil fruit. A sound tree cannot bear evil fruit, nor a bad tree bear good fruit [Matt. 7:17–18]."

Second, the admonition to change ourselves means that the change in us is already the beginning of the change in the world and the strategy for changing the world: "You are the salt of the earth. . . . You are the light of the world [Matt. 5:13–14]"; "So we are ambassadors for Christ, God making God's own appeal through us. [2 Cor. 5:20]."

The mandate for change is contained in the dynamics of the gift and the promise. The gift is the new reality of God's grace and holiness that confronts us to our surprise and bewilderment. It confronted Moses in the call to go down to Egypt; it is the presence of God, which declared to Israel: "I am the Lord your God, who brought you out of the land of Egypt [Exod. 20:2]." The gift is given to Mary, who declares: "My soul magnifies the Lord, and my spirit rejoices in God my Savior [Luke 1:46–47]." It is embodied in Jesus' announcement of the presence of God's reign.

The promise is the assurance that we shall become what we are in God's sight:

> You have seen what I did to the Egyptians, and how I bore you on eagles' wings and brought you to myself. Now therefore, if you will obey my voice and keep my covenant, you shall be my own possession among all peoples; for all the earth is mine, and you shall be to me a kingdom of priests and a holy nation.
>
> —Exodus 19:4–6

The same covenantal promise is expressed in Zechariah's prophecy in Luke 1:67–79 and Jesus' reading from Isaiah:

The Spirit of the Lord is upon me,
because God has anointed me to preach good news to the poor.
God has sent me to proclaim release to the captives
and recovering of sight to the blind,
to set at liberty those who are oppressed,
to proclaim the acceptable year of the Lord.

—Luke 4:18–19

Both the gift and the promise confer the new reality and the possibility for change. But there is a priority to the gift and an open-endedness to the promise. The gift is eternally rooted in the love of God and always contains the promise; the promise grows out of the gift and invites us to become what God wills us to be in Christ. The one is the foundation for our new life; the other is the call to be changed.

The relation of gift and promise is parallel to the traditional language of justification and sanctification. These two technical terms were developed by Paul and have become the basic categories for understanding the gift and the promise in Christian life. The term *justification* is a legal and moral declaration of acceptability. Applied to our relation to God, Paul declared that we have standing in the presence of God by God's grace and not by any claim of our own. The sinner, who has no claim to stand on, is justified by grace (Romans 5:1–5). By contrast, the promise of renewal is termed *sanctification*, which simply means to make sacred or holy. Whereas justification points to that foundation of trust in the love of God, sanctification points to the open future God sets before us, wherein we may become the people of God.

The distinction is not new to Paul but is deeply rooted in Israel's experience that the covenant is grounded in the love of God and is a call to be holy as God is holy. It would be an outright denial of grace and an act of pride to suggest that we can or must be sanctified before we are justified. Such a position may be called legalism, for it assumes our standing before God depends on our fulfillment of the promise before we receive the gift. It denies that the promise is always given in the gift and grows out of the gift. While legalism has repeatedly been rejected in theory, it constantly reappears in every generation's practice.

The Christian tradition has been quite clear on the logical order of justification and sanctification. The gift always precedes and contains the promise; the promise is always contained in and mandated by the gift. What is not as clear is the definition of the promise. What is to be expected of us once we receive the gift? And what can we expect of God on our behalf?

The Fear of Change

One of the reasons we seldom ask or answer these questions of expectations is our fear of change. But why would anyone fear the change that brings new life? Is not grace irresistible?

Consider an image drawn from fiction, in the cinematic version of *Ironweed*. In this story Jack Nicholson plays the role of a man fleeing his past for some twenty years. He lives on the streets of Albany, New York, sharing the many hardships and few joys of those down and out during the depression. He left his family because while drunk he caused the death of his infant son. His flight represents his self-contempt as well as his inability to face his wife and two other children. Then during a chance meeting with his other son, now grown, his son tells him: "Mother doesn't blame you." This revelation of grace only causes the man greater confusion and terror. He cannot believe that anyone could act in such a way, since the world that he experiences is hostile and judgmental to those who fail. But one senses that what really prevents the man from facing this word of reconciliation is fear. Grace lays a claim upon us and draws us into a community of hope and care. It obligates us and places expectations upon us. It is indeed terrifying, even more than the self-hatred, more than the loneliness and misery of the cold streets.

Do we resist the grace of God because we know full well that the One who claims us with such love also wills us to be renewed in and with other people? The power of the gift (justification) is precisely its ability to reveal the new possibilities (sanctification). Our reconciliation with God and neighbor; the mind of Christ as faith, hope, and love; and the gifts of freedom, joy, and gratitude—all are real possibilities. Grace is the character of life-giving power bestowed upon us in the midst of our need. Grace of necessity points to the new life contained in the intervention of love.

To speak of a grace that contains no promise of new life, that points to no reconciliation, that bestows no new mind is to misunderstand the divine purpose. This is not to void the loving intention of God, making God's action dependent upon some anticipated human response. Christ made it clear in word and action that the divine love is an eternal and unlimited willingness to give life. It is precisely such love that contains the promise. But to speak of a grace that points to no promise is, as Dietrich Bonhoeffer argued, a cheap grace. It is to suggest that Christ paid no price for his faithfulness to God. It is to suggest that we can celebrate being God's chosen people and ignore the promise contained in such a gift. Cheap grace makes no demands, utters no call, speaks no words of discipline, asks for no change. Cheap grace stands the gospel of costly grace on its head in the illusion that we can be truly human without being changed.

But if we reconnect sanctification with justification, the promise with the gift, will we not lapse into the worst form of legalism and destroy the very gospel we seek to proclaim? Such a question represents the misunderstanding in our own selves regarding the relation of the promise to the gift. It assumes that the promise is really a new requirement to be achieved prior to receipt of the gift. It assumes that receiving the promise will be a new source of personal claim, dividing us from one another. The question can be removed from our concern only by clarifying the relation of the gift and the promise in the new being of Jesus Christ.

The New Being in Jesus Christ

The church year is a resource for our spiritual renewal. It speaks to us of events rather than ideas. It confronts us with three decisive moments: Christmas, Good Friday to Easter, and Pentecost. All of the other periods in the liturgical year either announce or flow from these events. In each case the quiet of the status quo is broken, and people are confronted with a divine presence so overwhelming that it is both a judgment and a gift of life.

At Christmas the world is surprised to find a birth, which is the sign of peace on earth. But it is not as everyone expected, as we see in the discomfort of Mary and Joseph, Zechariah and Elizabeth, Herod the king and the wisemen. There is no place for this child, Zechariah becomes mute, a fearful king conspires to kill the child, innocent children are slaughtered, and the parents flee in the night. Mary, using the words of Hannah, the mother of Samuel, praises God for the coming salvation, which will reverse the claims of this world and restore the lives of those persons in need. Zechariah blesses the Lord God for the divine faithfulness and the coming deliverance. An old man Simeon and an old prophetess Anna give thanks for God's redemption of all peoples.

In Jesus' entrance into Jerusalem the people are confronted by his uncompromising proclamation of the rule of God—an event that challenged the current claims to righteousness and the very nature of the spiritual community. While those in power are threatened by Jesus' words and presence, his disciples continue to be confused in their expectations of Jesus and their response to him. Jesus is rejected, condemned, and crucified. After this series of events, which the disciples could not anticipate or control, Jesus is resurrected, which again confounds the human powers and expectations. The crucified is made Lord as a sign of the salvation of all people.

Before Pentecost the disciples gather together in Jerusalem. They are given a new confidence by the appearance of Jesus and await the baptism of the Holy Spirit. They reconstitute their membership of twelve by choosing Matthias to replace Judas. But questions of power and the future appear unresolved: "Lord, will you at this time restore the kingdom to Israel [Acts 1:6]?" At the bestowal of the Spirit, they begin to speak in other tongues, so that people from many nations "hear them telling in our own tongues the mighty works of God [Acts 2:11]." Could God's intervention to empower the disciples as witnesses to the whole world be more striking! Do we not have here a reversal of the disaster created in the story of the Tower of Babel, where the languages of the nations were confused because of the arrogant attempt to storm heaven by human power and wisdom? The inability to understand one another, the ancient symbol of difference and separation, is now broken down through the bestowal of the Spirit.

Then there is even a bit of comic relief. When the disciples are accused of being drunk—how else would one explain this event according to worldly wisdom?—Peter responds that this could not be the case because it is still morning. But Peter has more to say. He presents a powerful sermon, retelling the events of the past months. The listeners are confronted by their own state of loss and ask: "Brethren, what shall we do [Acts 2:37]?"

In all three events, human trust and loyalty are confronted by a presence that reveals both power and goodness and summons faith to choose God's cause. Jesus appears as a child forsaken and then as a man proclaiming the realm of God. Jesus is present to his disciples as one crucified and risen. The Holy Spirit is present in them, as the very Spirit of God. The Spirit is the promise of God (Acts 1:5) and an enabling power to witness to Christ the Lord (Acts 2:36). The new being that enlivens the early Christians is not an idea, an ethical teaching, or a strategy for action. It is first a presence. This fact must become the starting point in our discussion of sanctification (that is, what we are to be and do).

The promise regarding our future is always connected with the gift present in our midst. Two references make this clear. Matthew 28 gives us the story leading to the Great Commission, to go forth into all the world. The command to do something is connected with Jesus' presence and his promise. Jesus first appears and is present with his disciples. The command is not given from afar or through impersonal means. They are then sent forth with the promise of his presence: "Lo, I am with you always, to the close of the age [Matt. 28:20]." Even the command itself is connected to Jesus' presence. They are to baptize in the name of God, the Father, Son, and Holy Spirit. Baptism is our incorporation into the Body of Christ, our death and resurrection with Jesus. The command to do something is, therefore, at every point a calling to faithfulness in the presence of Christ.

The second reference to the gift is made by Paul. In 1 and 2 Corinthians, Paul makes it clear that the basis for any new life is the Spirit of God (1 Corinthians 2:10–13; 3:16). New possibilities are not demands placed upon us that must be achieved prior to acceptance by God or membership in the church community. This ethic of the gift is even reflected in Paul's criticism. The logic of his critical remarks is that the Corinthians have not acted in ways consistent with the gift. In effect, Paul's feeling is expressed in the cry, When will you be what you already are? They are like infants, unable to take solid food, and so Paul must speak to them as infants rather than as mature persons (1 Corinthians 3:1–4).

For Paul, the fact is that an event has occurred that creates the new context for all questions of thinking and doing: Christ has died for all that they might live no longer for themselves but for Christ (2 Corinthians 5:15). In verses 16 and 17, Paul captures the essence of this life in the presence of the promise: "From now on, therefore, we regard no one from a human point of view; even though we once regarded Christ from a human point of view, we regard him thus no longer. Therefore, if any one is in Christ, that one is a new creation; the old has passed away, behold, the new has come." A change has taken place, and we now live in the presence of the Spirit of Christ. We are to become what we are in the new creation.

Both Matthew 28 and the Corinthian references make clear that *what we are to become and how it is possible* are already given in the gift. Sanctification is not something unrelated or beyond the gift but occurs in the context of our new identity and status in the presence of

Christ. It is the promise of what God wills for us. But it is always in
the gift itself, and the gift creates the context for daring to hope and
think about the promise. An old slogan given to seminarians years ago
stated: "The indicative always precedes the imperative." That means
for us that the command to do something always comes after the
statement of fact regarding our new life in Christ. Biblical faith does
not say do such and such and then you will be accepted. Instead it
affirms the gift and offers a promise: God loves you; now become what
you are in Christ.

If we take the command out of the new reality created by the gift,
then the command looms large as a threatening requirement. We are
faced with a most difficult problem. Our standing before God and
neighbor is dependent on fulfillment of the command, but the
command is impossible. This dilemma has produced a variety of
responses. (1) Rationalism is the most optimistic one, which sees in
the radical character of the command a purity that is evidence of
Jesus' teachings. (2) Despair is the opposite reaction, evoked at the
impossibility of fulfilling the command. For many Christians such
despair is avoided by simply ignoring the command. (3) A grand
compromise was developed in the medieval period by creating a two-
story world of religious orders and laity. The full force of the
command fell only on the religious orders; the laity were not expected
to live the higher life of obedience, poverty, and celibacy. All three
responses create in their own way innumerable tensions and unresolved contradictions. Only if we place the command in the new
reality of the gift are we able to see the command as a promise for us.

Christian Being: Becoming What We Are in Christ

If the promise of our future is reconnected to the gift, this means
that the content of the promise is already given in the gift and that
the new life is made possible by the same Spirit that bestowed the gift.
Sanctification then appears as the process whereby we are recreated by
and in the mind of Christ. Its agenda is not, in its general direction,
subject to debate or waiting to be developed. We need to return again
and again to the gift and allow ourselves to be reformed by the mind
of Christ. As an expression of this conviction, we return to Paul's
triad of faith, hope, and love, as the general form and content of the
mind of Christ in us. Each is a gift of new life, planted like a seed in

us, which must grow up in the very special space that constitutes our existence.

Faith

To place one's faith in God is to affirm that God is the source of all things but, more personally, that God is the source of one's life. It is to rely upon God in the certainty that God is trustworthy. The practice of such faith is twofold.

First, faith is knowing that this holy One revealed to Israel and in the person of Jesus Christ is God. To use Paul's phrase "from now on, therefore," all other acts of trust and loyalty are reordered. Such reassessment does not mean the total rejection of things in this world. To trust God is not to choose either God or the world. Nor is it to conduct periodic scanning tests on our religious life to determine if we love God at least 51 percent more than people and places of the creation. Instead, all things in our lives and the world are revalued as they become part of the Rule of God. This is what it means to reorient ourselves, to center all things, including ourselves, in God. Such centering involves the paradox of losing and finding, which Jesus presents to the disciples. To love all things in God is in one sense to lose them, for they are no longer our possessions, nor are they the objects that give us ultimate worth. They are limited in their claim upon us and our investment in them because they are not God, and our ultimate trust and loyalty can only be to God. But they are given back to us as part of the creation to be loved in God. They are valued because they are gifts of God's love to us, to sustain and ennoble human life.

Second, faith is knowing that we are individually and communally named by God. It is to know with certainty that we are valued and that God wills each of us to be an image of the new creation. Such faith bestows a confidence born of the Spirit that our lives are eternally in the presence of Christ. Only from such a vantage point can we begin to reorder our lives. In Christ things fall into their proper place instead of falling apart, the common experience. Personal integrity and wholeness are derived from the clarity that comes from knowing ourselves in the presence of God. How can the parts be re-formed into a harmonious whole without a principle of order? Such an order is the gift of being members of God's Rule.

This twofold practice of faith in God is captured in the image of "living without claims." By this we mean the willingness to step outside of the attempt to be self-sufficient and of the endless battle of defensiveness. It is to rely upon God. Such a life without claims is simultaneously exhilarating and terrifying. It is exhilarating to be freed from the burden of claims and the demands of worldly wisdom. There is no liberation more joyful than the discovery that God is God and that we are bound together in the people of God.

But the practice of such faith is also terrifying. An autonomous world expects us to create ourselves and entrust ourselves to material and social powers. It resists and even shuns the faith that frees us from such pressures. It is threatened by anyone at rest or peace, who dares to live without claims, since the world requires assertion and defensiveness. Even our own anxieties cause us to doubt that God is the true source of life and will fulfill the promise to us. It is not simply the power of the autonomous world that threatens us; our own powerlessness terrifies us. Such doubt can only be overcome by returning to the gift and the promise. Thus faith requires deliberate practice: hearing the good news of the gift; reassessing our acts of trust and loyalty; affirming ourselves as people of God; and allowing the Spirit to actualize the new creation in us.

When we speak of such faith and its practice, it is self-evident that faith necessarily expresses itself in acts of witness. In one sense, to ask, How shall we witness to faith? is redundant. If a person trusts in God and affirms that he or she is a member of God's realm, freed from the powers of the world, that person is already witnessing to faith. Such a person already stands out like a light in a dark night. It is a revolutionary thing to trust in God and be named by God, revolutionary in the sense that one has been turned around and demonstrates such turning to others. In a world of multiple causes that devalue people and claim too much for themselves, the person who trusts in God is already a witness. What is needed, therefore, is not general discussions about the broad direction of our witness but the specific application of such faith to where we are in our lives. Our task is not to reinvent the gospel; we already have the commission to baptize in the name of God. Our task is to open our eyes and ears to a world of pain and conflicting claims and to determine how faith in God requires reassessment and re-creation. This is the witness of faith: to allow ourselves to be shaped by the gift and to trust that the promise for new life can and will be actualized in us.

Love

The gift places us in the new reality of being loved: of being claimed and valued, of being under the care of One whose love knows no limits. The gift contains the promise that we are enabled to love.

To understand this we must recall our analysis of life in the world of claims, self-assertion, and defensiveness. It is not an easy thing to be free from the preoccupation with ourselves. The endless search for acceptance and care of oneself is like a blindness that prevents us from seeing other people as people with real needs and concerns. The preoccupation with ourselves creates in us the fear that any expenditure of time, energy, or possessions is a negative cash balance, a depletion of what we have and what we are. We are not able to love until we are freed from the confines of exclusive views that define our world as a fortress to be protected from outside interference. But the gift means the freedom from such bondage. It is, as John's Gospel tells us in the story of Nicodemus, to be born again, to be in the presence of God, now seeing all people and the world as parts of God's creation. To be a new creation in Christ is to receive the will and the power to love.

Here we must begin by applying the promise to ourselves. If God is gracious to us, then perhaps we can begin by being gracious to ourselves. This is said in light of our analysis of autonomous and moral life, wherein the self lives under the demand to be worthy and the strain of self-criticism. It is also said in light of the stream of data reporting that so many people lack a positive self-image or self-confidence. People who suffer severe emotional distress, abuse alcohol and other drugs, are trapped in domestic violence, or are unable to pursue career goals reveal an underlying theme. They do not feel good about themselves. They appear to be victims of a competitive society that withholds approval from individuals as well as large groups (e.g., minorities and women). But the promise is that one can be freed from this exile, whether it is self-imposed or imposed by society. In the first instance, the gift means to love oneself and care for oneself as a member of God's people.

What would it mean to be gracious to ourselves? In a society that denies value to so many people on the basis of wealth, status, education, ability, or performance, the possibilities are unlimited. Moreover, when we consider the offers society makes for ways to be gracious to ourselves, we are again confronted with serious problems.

They include unlimited acquisition of possessions, over-indulgence of food and drink, the misuse of sexuality, and entertainment often too costly to ourselves and society. In such a world, receiving the promsie requires of us time to sort out our true identity from the many false ones. Above all, it requires the practice of remembering who we are in the presence of God and of being together in the community of the gift. In hearing the proclamation of grace, in prayer and worship, in the openness of friendship and rigorous self-assessment inspired by the gift, the Spirit actualizes the promise in each of us.

The promise also means that we shall be free and able to love one another, to engage in a ministry of reconciliation. Once more such a promise must be understood against the background of a world that knows little genuine community. In our culture we have seen the rise of an individualism that appears incapable of genuine intimacy or personal trust, because other people are seen as threats to the identity and worth of the self. Friendship, marriage, or children all appear to be imposed on the time or resources of the individual. We have seen class and race tensions escalate, reflecting age-old systems of exclusion and repression. The nations of our world engage in war as the simplest means of achieving political ends, or create divisions that become arenas for the endless cycle of blood vengeance. We see this in Northern Ireland, Lebanon, Israel, South Africa, and Latin America. It is in the face of this alienation and warfare that grace is both a priceless gift and a promise. To be claimed by God's love is to receive the promise that we shall be able to overcome our fear and turn to others in acts of grace.

Although we are repeatedly tempted to live our lives in an imaginary dreamland, those who wish to practice the promise of love must stay close to the reality of life, where there is genuine pain and joy. For example, the parents of a young man who died of cancer described their life together in his last years. He was an energetic and enthusiastic person. He refused to allow his illness to limit him or to become an object of sympathy. After years of suffering and great joy he died. His mother and father spoke of the deep pain they felt, as well as the great joy and satisfaction they knew through this special son. They spoke of how they were befriended and supported by family and friends. But they also mentioned how some people could not deal with their son and his death, because the crisis was too fearful. After his death even the parents began to wonder if they should talk to people about their son, because it made others uncomfortable. They were tempted to be silent. They even asked themselves if they should tell their story to other families who had seriously ill children, lest telling it increase the others' anxieties. The parents resolved to be with others who suffered such terrible pain and, in being with them, to speak of the love they have received.

This case illustrates how we are tempted by a fearful world to lose touch with reality. The world would have us believe that we will live forever, that no one dies, that there is no suffering, that there is no cross and certainly no resurrection. It would have us believe that the context for life is consumption, winning, ruling over others, and being secure in our claims. Reality is covered up and hidden by Hollywood and Las Vegas, by dreams of winning the lottery, and by the illusion of security in financial and military power.

But the gift declares that reality involves crisis and crucifixion. Reality consists of the simple gifts of food and rest, honest speech, and acts of sharing. Reality consists of people who are lonely, who are in great pain, and who die. Those who would seek the promise of love must stay close to the reality of the world, for it is in this real world that the gift is given.

The promise of love as a ministry of reconciliation, which Paul speaks of in 2 Corinthians 5, is a promise that is made possible by the the gift itself. It is not a *work* we are to do through our own ingenuity and planning. It is a possibility because it declares that God—the creator of all that is—has created a common ground on which all of us may stand. This common ground is not the elimination of individuality or the interests of each person or group. It is not the victory of the most powerful side, so that the minority is asked to become like the majority. When Paul declares that we are reconciled in Christ, he means that our union is a gift of God, grounded not in your or my design but in God's will that we live in peace.

To love, therefore, means simply to listen again and again to the good news of the gift of our reunion in God's grace, to reassess the dividing lines in light of this new reality, and to allow the Spirit to work in us as agents of reconciliation. It is to believe that the promise is to us and to our children: that life can be made whole, that we can actually live together in bonds of trust, that fidelity is not the loss of freedom but its highest expression, that the walls of separation can be broken down and replaced with the peace of God. All these things are the practice of God's love in us.

Hope

To receive the gift of new being in Jesus Christ is to be allowed to hope in the promises of God. Such hope is not the work of an idle imagination, but the earnest expectation that the promise is for us wherever we are. Hope is not an exercise that proves our endurance or special commitment. Christian hope is the direct consequence of the gift of grace. Those who trust in God and receive the love of God are given the expectation that God will redeem the world. It is for this reason that we have placed hope after faith and love. It is the consequence of our trust in God and the Spirit in us.

But for what can we hope? While driving in Pennsylvania I encountered a roadside billboard with the words "Pray. It works." This claim to the efficacy of prayer in the midst of numerous other advertisements appeared to be typical of American pragmatism. Religion is defined as something we do for our benefit, when and where we choose. It is presented, defined, and evaluated in terms of what it will do for us. So, in a world where our needs are unlimited and where we have tried so many other strategies, cures, and remedies, and a host of how-to self-improvement programs, here was but one more offer. Why not give prayer a chance?

As you can well imagine, this sign provoked in me a storm of protest. Jesus repeatedly admonishes his followers against the dangers of self-serving petitions and hypocrisy in prayer and even gives them a model prayer. In his own life he prays, "Yet not what I will, but what thou wilt." The God of the Bible is the Creator of heaven and earth. God is not an idol or a magical power to be manipulated by human interests. The Old Testament prohibition against taking the name of the Lord in vain and the ban on idols are parts of a general rejection of trying to use God for our purposes or redefining God's purposes for our use. The same perspective is embodied in Jesus' insistence that it is the Rule of God that is at hand.

The concern about making God into a spiritual mail-order catalogue service is more than a theoretical one. Our age has witnessed people seeking to bless every cause, no matter how exclusive or oppressive. In recent years we have witnessed the abuses by some of television's religious programs: raising money for private gain and broadcasting scandalous theology. They assume that religion is for people's needs, that God will meet every need, and that the only thing required is a request, or "faith." This is idolatry. It makes everything depend on human action: God will not do anything until you believe; God will do what you want. Perhaps the most tragic consequence of this is the effect upon the people truly distressed and physically sick. They are drawn into a logic that can only conclude that if they are not healed, it is because they lack true faith. Guilt is added to their pain.

But in spite of these corruptions of prayer and hope, what can we ask of God? We can ask for precisely what God has promised. In fact, Jesus teaches his disciples to petition God. Like a father who will not respond with a stone to a child's request for bread, God will respond lovingly to our petitions. God has promised freedom from the idols and demonic powers of this world, daily bread, the forgiveness of sins, the knowledge of being named by God, reconciliation with one another, the healing of the sick, the resurrection of the dead, and peace on earth.

The scope of the promise is overwhelming, to be sure. Some of the things are so far beyond our expectations that we easily dismiss them, typical of our worldly wisdom. We have allowed the world to define what is possible and impossible, and we have even internalized such values through our fears that what God has promised cannot happen. So, when a person is kind or supportive, we are surprised and wonder why he or she is that way. When secular world leaders reach a breakthrough on peace, we are astonished and wonder what has happened. What a sad commentary that it then becomes permissible to speak of peace! Is not our real problem that we have not practiced the hope derived from the gift? We have not trusted in the God of the promise to actualize in us the divine will.

Hope rests on what God has already given and promised. The practice of hope, therefore, returns again and again to the gift and the promise. Hope is an act of trust in God and an expression of our love for God and the world. In hope we allow the Spirit to awaken us to new possibilities. This is not a trick of autosuggestion. It is submitting oneself to the discipline of reassessing our expectations in light of God's promises. It is an act of reordering our lives in accordance with the reconciling love of God.

Why have we not mentioned the gifts of freedom, joy, and gratitude in this discussion of the promise? Although these are part of what we are to become in Christ, the issue is not whether we *want* to be free, joyful, or grateful. Desiring them cannot produce them. Such states are not something we create. They are the result of the new creation. We are free when we are liberated from false claims and oppressive powers. We are free when we are rescued from our alienation and loneliness and when we are willing to risk friendship and community. In a similar way, we do not decide to be happy or grateful. We are joyful and grateful, because something causes us to rejoice and affirm the creative powers at work in the world. The mind of Christ is indeed marked by freedom, joy, and gratitude, but only because it is rooted in the gift and the promises of God.

The question was posed: What shall we become as Christians? Our answer is "To become what we already are in the gift of Jesus Christ."

> So if there is any encouragement in Christ, any incentive of love, any participation in the Spirit, any affection and sympathy, complete my joy by being of the same mind, having the same love, being in full accord and of one mind. Do nothing from selfishness or conceit, but in humility count others better than yourselves. Let each of you look not only to your own interests, but also to the interests of others. Have this mind among yourselves, which you have in Christ Jesus, who, though in the form of God, did not count equality with God a thing to be grasped, but emptied himself, taking the form of a servant, being born in the likeness of human beings. And being found in human form, Christ humbled himself and became obedient unto death, even death on a cross. Therefore God has highly exalted him and bestowed on him the name which is above every name, that at the name of Jesus every knee should bow, in heaven and on earth and under the earth, and every tongue confess that Jesus Christ is Lord, to the glory of God the Father.
>
> Therefore, my beloved, as you have always obeyed, so now, not only as in my presence but much more in my absence, work out your own salvation with fear and trembling; for God is at work in you, both to will and to work for God's good pleasure.
>
> Do all things without grumbling or questioning.
>
> —Philippians 2:1–14

Summary

We have affirmed that the gift of God's love in Jesus Christ contains within it the promise of new life. In this sense, the gift always points to the new reality God would have us become, and God's promises are always rooted in the gift. To trust God is, therefore, to open ourselves to the transforming power of God.

When we reconnect the promise of new life with the gift of God's love, then we must ask: Who is it that God would have us be? This question must be answered in this way: to become who we are in Christ. The gift itself contains the transforming power of God. It inspires personal and social change. The Christian life and the life of the church are therefore governed—as they should be—by the mind of Christ. We trust (i.e., have faith) in God through Christ; we hope in God's promises through Christ; and we love as we have been loved, through Christ.

Issues for Reflection and Discussion

1. Give some thought to the matter of your personal expectations in your religious life: For what do you hope? Do you expect any change in yourself? When was the last time you asked God for something?
2. If hope for change has not been a part of your religious life, how would you explain this? Are there any fears or barriers to hoping for change?
3. Is the analysis of fear of change a reality in the life of your congregation? When was the last time the congregation set a goal or expressed a hope?
4. Try to think of the promise in its most simple and personal form. What happens if you reflect upon the gift and the promise in light of what is most important to you?
5. To what extent have you thought of social justice issues as part of the promise? Is there any connection between your personal needs or expectations and larger social issues? Does viewing social issues in light of the promise change your perspective with respect to what is important or what is possible?

Bibliography

I Corinthians

Barrett, C. K. A *Commentary on the First Epistle to the Corinthians*. 2nd ed. London: Adam and Charles Black, 1971.

Conzelman, Hans. A *Commentary on the First Epistle to the Corinthians*. Translated by James W. Leitch. Philadelphia: Fortress Press, 1975.

Koester, Helmut. *Introduction to the New Testament*. 2 vols. Philadelphia: Fortress Press, 1982.

Kummel, W. G. *Introduction to the New Testament*. rev. ed. Translated by A. J. Mattill, Jr. London: SCM Press, Ltd., 1966.

Pearson, Birger A. *The Pneumatikos-Psychikos Terminology in I Corinthians*. Missoula, Montana: Scholars Press, 1973.

Schmithals, Walter. *Gnosticism in Corinth: An Investigation of the Letters to the Corinthians*. Translated by John E. Steeley. Nashville: Abingdon Press, 1971.

H. Richard Niebuhr

Fowler, James W. *To See The Kingdom: The Theological Vision of H. Richard Niebuhr*. Nashville: Abingdon Press, 1974.

Niebuhr, H. Richard. *The Kingdom of God in America*. New York: Harper & Brothers, 1959.

———. *The Meaning of Revelation*. New York: The Macmillan Co., 1941.

———. *Radical Monotheism and Western Culture, with Supplementary Essays*. New York: Harper & Row, Publishers, 1960.

————. *The Responsible Self.* Harper and Row, Publishers, 1963.

Ransey, Paul (ed.). *Faith and Ethics: The Theology of H. Richard Niebuhr.* New York: Harper and Row, Publishers, 1957.

General

Bunyan, John. *The Pilgrim's Progress.* Edited by Roger Sharrock. Harmondsworth, England: Penguin Books Inc., 1965.

Dillenberger, John (ed.). *Martin Luther: Selections from His Writings.* Garden City, New York: Doubleday & Co., Inc., 1961.

Miller, Allen O., and Osterhaven, M. Eugene (eds.). *The Heidelberg Catechism.* New York: United Church Press, 1962.

Silone, Ignazio. *Bread and Wine.* New York: New American Library, 1963.

Notes

Notes

Notes

The Gift and the Promise

Becoming What We Are in Christ

Leader's Guide

Peter Schmiechen

Kaleidoscope Series Resource

United Church Press
New York

Before you read this manual . . .

This Leader's Guide has been prepared as a resource for the teacher of this Kaleidoscope course. However, you may wish to read the text before you read the Leader's Guide in order to see the text with the same eyes as will the members of the class. Such a reading will give you the opportunity to make marginal comments and will also make the guide more understandable, since it is a commentary on the text.

Introduction to the Leader's Guide

Welcome to Kaleidoscope. This course has been prepared by Lancaster Theological Seminary and the United Church Press of the United Church of Christ. It is a course of study for adults seeking to grow in faith and self-understanding. It does not require that you have prior courses. The Kaleidoscope Series offers other courses, however, which we hope you and members of your congregation will consider using.

The series grew out of a program for adults at Lancaster Seminary. The most common characteristic among those people in attendance was *a general interest in the particular course,* rather than age, gender, work experience, or education. Similarly, the persons taking your course will probably be highly motivated for the subject of Christian growth, while reflecting a wide range of backgrounds and interests.

Who should lead this course? In designing these courses, we assumed that you, the leader, would share the interest of the class in this particular subject and be able to—

• be at ease with new ideas;
• commit time for careful reading;
• facilitate open discussion (this includes the ability to help the class see key ideas, relate them to their experience, and ask questions);
• have the patience to live with silence, to allow the class to reflect, and to wait for the class to respond.

It is not required that you be ordained or have theological training. If you do possess these gifts, however, they will certainly be of use in leading the course.

The Purpose and Outline of the Course

In this course I propose to develop a model of conversion based on the concepts of crisis and reorientation. The general thesis is that conversion creates a new form of identity and self-worth, derived from the experience of crisis. Becoming Christian is primarily the experience that identity and self-worth are gifts rather than achievements. This general thesis, developed specifically in Christian terms, begins with Paul and the experience of the cross as the primary meaning of crisis. Reorientation to life after a crisis is developed in terms of the gift and the promise of God in Jesus Christ.

This thesis is grounded on two convictions: first, that *becoming* Christian is a turning away from something to something; second, that *becoming* and *being* Christian are so intertwined that it is impossible to distinguish them. We continue to confess that we are still in the process of becoming, yet we also acknowledge that God has already claimed us and is working within us. These two assumptions allow us to speak of conversion as a radical change and as a process that is lifelong.

The first four chapters form a unit: the basic analysis and theory about becoming Christian. Chapter 5 allows the class to engage in reflection exercises as a way of understanding and applying the model of crises and reorientation to their lives. Chapter 6 concludes the course by focusing on the promise contained in God's gift. It thus highlights that becoming Christian is a lifelong process.

Theology and Its Relation to the Christian Life

A word about theology, as we begin to work together in this enterprise: Christian theology is confession and reflection on our being in the presence of God through Jesus Christ. Allow me to unravel this statement.

First, theology is not God, the Bible, or our faith. It is a thoughtful action upon and about our Christian life. This definition frees us from the arrogant view that what we formulate theologically is absolutely equal to God, who is always the sovereign Lord, far greater and more gracious than we can imagine. While theology gives us the freedom to ask questions about the Christian life, it does not create faith, nor can it destroy faith. Faith is the gift of the Spirit in response to God's gracious activity. Faith does not rest on our theology (thank God) but on the goodness of God. So we attempt to describe God and ask questions about God (good ones and some that seem stupid). We sometimes succeed in reaching clarity, and sometimes we fail. The clarifying process is begun in faith, in the confidence that God will renew our minds and our hearts.

Second, theology is both confession and reflection. The two are inseparable and impact upon each other. The Bible reveals a natural and necessary desire to confess who God is and what God has done. At the same time, the confession is affected by serious reflection, which asks difficult questions and confronts our confession with our own doubt and confusion. For example, Jesus uses parables and teachings to clarify general confessions that are already known. The parables offer a type of reflection in light of current needs, tensions, and conflicts.

Finally, Christian theology exists in the service of the gospel of Christ. It arises out of the life of the church in this world, with all of the struggles and pain inside the church and throughout the world. It seeks to serve the church by its confession of God as the One revealed in Israel and in Jesus Christ. It serves the church by asking serious questions about our faith and action. It claims no authority other than that of the gospel. Its service to the church is offered for the sake of the church's life and as a witness in the world.

From this brief statement about theology we can draw two conclusions regarding the teaching of this course. One is that theology is a personal issue. We speak out of personal faith with commitment—and sometimes passion. Contrary to popular images of people in ivory towers studying abstract theories, theologians can easily find themselves in the midst of serious debate. This course asks laypeople to examine their situation and speak from their hearts.

The second conclusion is that process is as important as content. If theology is dealing with confession and reflection about our being in the presence of God, then we must be personally involved in the process. The class procedure will therefore emphasize participation by class members in addition to you as leader transmitting the material.

Comments on the Methods of This Course

We have already indicated several significant values that govern the methodology of this course. Here we add several more that have shaped the material.

The intersections of life. Christian theology deals with a variety of polarities, or relations, that intersect in the life of the believer: God and the world, the reader and the text, the church and the world, reflection and worship, quietude and action. These polarities are all part of our lives, and they become the context for our theological work. This fact complicates our task.

We do not look at a text in isolation from these multiple subjects. Shall we speak of conversion by starting with the solitary individual or with his or her world? Do we start with God or with human life? Shall we talk about Paul or today's newspaper? We will have to talk about all of these things, because all are a part of our lives. All affect us and the way we do theology. The course, therefore, moves back and forth between the individual and society, the church and the world, the solitary self and its relation to other people as well as to God.

Repetition. Much education proceeds from the simple to the complex or moves from one point to a new point. We, however, use a different approach. We begin with complex things and stay with them. To be sure, the complex subject of faith in God can be broken down into parts. But theology is more a plunge into deep water than a step into a wading pool. Moreover, we do not get beyond the original starting point. I confess that I have been working on some issues for twenty to thirty years. They are the issues all of us consider: for example, what is love and how is it related to justice? Theology starts at one point and tends to stay there.

If starting with a complex subject seems frightening, the saving grace is repetition. In this course we repeat quite deliberately. A theme is announced, analyzed in parts, repeated, viewed from new perspectives, and reformulated. All the while the repetition allows us to see what was originally intended. Our understanding increases, because what is repeated is in one sense something quite new.

Repetition also allows group members to progress at different rates of speed, a process to be expected and respected. Because the theme is announced at the beginning and restated at the end, some people will understand it quickly at a basic level; others will discover gradually that the subject is far richer in substance than they ever imagined.

Personal involvement of the class. We have already noted that genuine theological discussion is personal. It speaks from faith to faith in search of greater understanding. At the same time, this course is not an attempt to convert members of the class. It is not a latter-day "anxious bench"—a nineteenth-century device employed to encourage religious conversion by having members sit on a bench before the congregation until something happened!

How then will you proceed with the class? My practice is to make it very clear that while we speak from faith, the purpose of the course is to increase our understanding. The class session is not a worship service, nor is the subject matter the text of a sermon. But the class does relate to worship and action, because it involves confession and reflection about our faith. Thus, class members must enter the dialogue as active participants.

Several things can facilitate participation. First, spend some time getting to know the class members, and allow them time to know one another. The arrangement of the class should facilitate personal involvement. A circle or square seating (so that they can see one another), a chalkboard for your use (which all can see), coffee and tea at the start or at a break period are all helpful. Second, take time to discover how people react to the text. Do they respond to theoretical ideas or to practical examples? Third, listen very carefully to what people say. Their comments before the class starts, their jokes about the subject or reading, their comments and silence in class, and their physical appearance become your data as a perceptive teacher. Fourth, ask people to expand on what they say. Most people will have encountered in ordinary language the broad options of Christian theology. Although they perceive the truth and feel great emotion about life, they have not spent time developing the analytic skills of expression. You can help them do so. Fifth, work at making connections among the sessions, overall course content, and common experience. Sixth, and finally, class discussion can be facilitated in many ways, including questions from you, questions from the class, or assignments to individuals to summarize a section.

One method for stimulating class discussion is to ask everyone to write, for five minutes, an answer to a question. The written response is to be kept by them—thereby eliminating test anxiety. The process of writing forces participants to express themselves. After everyone has written, ask for volunteers to tell what they wrote. The method also allows everyone to reflect upon what they wrote during and after a discussion. This exercise may expose a range of answers or confirm a person's ability to understand a difficult point.

In spite of all of its hazards, the teaching of theological subjects is a great adventure. The encounter of faith and life, the dialogue between persons, and the power of the gospel create a dynamic process. Indeed, teaching theology has always been something of a crisis for me: the discovery of myself in the presence of God and other persons, as well as new opportunities for turning. I know it will be such an opportunity for you. Give it your all, enjoy it, keep your eyes open, and above all, trust God.

Chapter 1: Turning

Main Objective

To understand how turning to God usually involves a crisis, wherein a particular event unveils what has been hidden and forces us to make a choice.

Basic Methods

1. Introduce the group to one another and become a class, be at ease, and focus attention on the educational goal.

2. View and discuss the video that introduces the author and three ways we become Christian.

3. Read and discuss 1 Corinthians 1–2; engage in serious biblical study.

Suggested Plan

1. *Prepare for the class.*

a. Before the first session, you will need to know where the class is to meet and who will attend. You then need to make arrangements for class members to receive a text, along with instructions to read chapter 1.

b. Prepare the classroom so that members can see and interact with one another, preferably seated around tables. They must also be able to see a chalkboard or newsprint easel and the video screen. It is best for seating and equipment to be set up in advance so you can move from discussion to blackboard or video without interruption or movement of the class.

c. Preview video spot #1, and determine how to introduce it and how to facilitate class discussion.

d. Write down for quick reference the instructions you want to give at the close of the class: reading assignments; questions for consideration; personal assignments. Prepare a prayer for the start of the class and/or make arrangements for the reading of scripture or the singing of a hymn.

2. *Begin the class.*

a. Introduce yourself, and ask the members to state their names and something about themselves. You may want to ask them to fill out a card with their name, telephone number, work, family situation, religious background, places of travel, favorite hobby, favorite movie or book in the last year, and so forth.

b. Offer your prayer, scripture, or hymn.

c. State why you agreed to teach this class and what you hope the group will be able to accomplish. You may want to ask members why they chose to attend this class.

3. *Show video spot #1.*

Ask the class what reactions they have to the three symbols in the chapel. Are these symbols decisive in their own processes of becoming Christian? What other symbols or events can they identify as part of this process? At this point your intention should be to highlight for the class some of these basic symbols but also to make clear that there are many ways people turn to God.

4. *Discuss chapter 1.*

a. At least an hour should be spent discussing chapter 1 and the material from 1 Corinthians. Remember that two sessions will be devoted to Paul. Be patient and let issues and questions emerge.

b. You will discover early in the process whether or not the class understands Paul and the analysis in the text. Some people will want to define the ideas and then proceed to their application; others will not understand Paul's logic until a good example is introduced. The section "The Cross as Symbol of Our Commonplace Experience" can be used early on or later in the discussion. Assess the situation and use your judgment. If what you do does not work, simply learn from it and bear that in mind for the next time. Teaching is an art, not a science. And remember we live by grace!

c. Focus on the main objective of the session. The summary at the close of the chapter and, following that, "Issues for Reflection and Discussion" allow you to focus the discussion. Try to assess whether members understand the numbered concepts in the summary. Time should be spent exploring these concepts, since they form the foundation for the entire course. The issues, in the form of questions, may provide a way into the concepts, allowing the class to apply the concepts to their own experience. Encourage the class to respond in their own words.

5. *Close the session.*

The class session should close after two hours with a clear directive from you. Do not let the class drag on so that some members leave before receiving reading instructions for session 2 (chapter 2). Make any other announcements about session 2, and wish the group well.

Chapter 2: The Gift

Main Objective

To complete the analysis of Paul's argument in 1 Corinthians and thereby come to a clear understanding of the way action proceeds out of being; the nature and consequence of human claims; God's gift of a new identity, membership in community, and the mind of Christ.

Basic Methods

1. Discuss chapter 2 and 1 Corinthians 1 and 2.
2. View and discuss video spot #2.

Suggested Plan

1. *Prepare for the class.*

a. Review the progress of session 1: Did the class understand the ideas and participate in the discussion? Determine if you need to backtrack to clarify any material. Do you need to take any special steps to involve all people in the discussion?

b. Prepare a prayer for opening the session.

c. Preview video spot #2.

d. Determine what instructions you will give at the close of the session.

2. *Welcome the class, and introduce any new members. Lead the class in prayer.*

3. *Ask for general reactions to the first session.*

4. *Outline the themes to be discussed:*
    a. Paul's logic as expressed in the diagram on page 13;
    b. The nature of claims;
    c. The gift.
5. *Ask for discussion regarding the diagram on page 13.* Do they understand it? Do they agree or disagree with its action flow? Can they give examples of its application?
6. *Introduce the section on claims.* Discuss the three subsections: origin, consequences, and loss of claims. Give examples or ask the class for examples.
7. At this point, perhaps fifty to sixty minutes into the session, *introduce video spot #2.* Ask for reactions.
8. *Now turn to the section "The Gift."* Ask how the gift differs from the life of claims.
9. *Close the session* by assessing progress and giving reading and any other procedural assignments for session 3.

Chapter 3: Expanding Our View of Faith

Main Objective

To enlarge our view of faith in two ways: (1) to understand faith as a social experience whereby we place trust and loyalty in a variety of objects or centers of value and by doing so create conflict between our many forms of faith; (2) to understand the Christian life as a continuous process of turning from limited objects of faith to the one true God.

Basic Methods

1. Discuss the analysis in chapter 3 of the theology of H. Richard Niebuhr and its application to the conversion process.
2. Examine certain Bible passages.
3. View and discuss video spot #3.

Suggested Plan

1. *Prepare for the class.*
    a. Review the progress made in the first two sessions to determine how much time is required for class discussion in this session.

   b. Prepare a prayer for opening the class.

   c. Preview video spot #3.

2. *Welcome the class and open the session with prayer.*

3. *Introduce the material from Niebuhr and its application in the chapter.*
Ask if the class has questions about the definitions. Work through the
basic concepts to assure a common understanding.

4. *Ask the class to apply the concepts or provide examples by responding to
the following questions:*

   a. How do they (the class) experience life parceled out to many
centers of value? Do they have divided loyalties?

   b. Have they experienced collision or loss?

   c. Is the idea of God as One who calls into question our limited
loyalties meaningful?

5. *Ask for reactions to the Bible passages listed on pages 32–33.*

6. *Show video spot #3, and discuss it.*

7. *Bring the class to a close and make the reading assignment for the next
session.*

Chapter 4: A Model of Conversion

Main Objective

To understand the model of conversion presented in the text and
use it to analyze our own experience.

Basic Methods

1. Discuss chapter 4, and apply its ideas to the class experience.

2. Use video spot #4, and discuss it. You may also use spot #5 in
this session, or save it for session 5.

Suggested Plan

1. *Prepare for the class.*

   a. Chapter 4 is the conclusion to the analysis and theory developed in chapters 1 through 3; therefore, this session ties together
the work done thus far. As you read chapter 4, note how it uses key
concepts developed in the earlier material. Take time to assess the
class's readiness for discussing the three-moment model. Do certain
concepts need review? Do more connections need to be made?

b. Preview video spot #4. This is an interview format, with two persons speaking of the experience of loss and control. The interview portrays two persons in transition, struggling with the crisis and the process of turning.

c. Prepare a prayer to open the session, and select a scripture passage or hymn.

d. Session 4 is intended to introduce the conceptual framework of the model of conversion. While examples and applications will help in this discussion, spend most of the time working through the model. Chapter 5 is devoted entirely to making practical applications using common experience, the Bible, and personal reflection. Survey chapter 5, and be prepared to give the group specific instructions as to how they should prepare for the next session.

2. *Welcome the class to the session, and open with prayer and scripture.*

3. *Introduce the topic for the session.* Remind the class that this session concludes the analysis started in chapter 1. Ask whether they see this connection.

4. *Review, outline, and discuss the "Three Moments in Life."*

a. Be sure the group understands how the concept of "moment" is being used.

b. Consider forming small groups of three to discuss the three moments together, or assign one moment to each group. Ask them to define the moments in their own words, give examples, and view them in terms of their own experience.

c. Review the progress made in understanding the three moments, especially as tools for personal understanding.

5. *At this point, you may want to use video spot #4.* The examples of crisis and turning will stimulate discussion.

6. *Consider the relations between the moments,* after the group is clear about the configuration of each moment. Why is it possible to live with more than one of these moments? Why do we move from one to another?

7. *Bring the class to a close, and give them instructions regarding the next session.* Note: Session 5 will focus on reflection exercises. Give a brief overview of chapter 5 and the purpose of the upcoming session. Ask for preferences regarding assignments, type of exercises used, and structuring of class time.

Chapter 5: Surveying the Contours and Boundaries of Our Hearts

Main Objective

To provide opportunity, encouragement, and assistance in reflecting upon our common experience and our own lives by means of the model of conversion.

Basic Methods

1. Use a variety of individual and group exercises (group discussion, small group conferences, written statements for personal use only, and personal reflection) so that each class member can use the model to gain greater self-understanding.

2. Use two video segments: interviews with two persons in the process of turning (spot #5), and commentary on the idols of commercial advertising (spot #6).

Suggested Plan

1. *Prepare for the class.*

a. Review chapter 5 in light of the discussion in session 4. Has the class understood the model? Is the class ready for a theology-in-action session?

If the answer is no, you may want to consider alternatives such as further review and discussion of chapters 1 to 4. But keep in mind that perhaps what is needed is the practical application provided for by chapter 5.

If the answer to the question you pose about understanding is yes, then assess how this class can best use the exercises of chapter 5, based on Bible passages, common experiences, and personal reflection. Although your class may not be able to do all the exercises, the variety of subjects illustrates the many applications of the model. Each person may engage in reflection at a point where he or she is comfortable. Therefore, give class members a choice in the use of the exercises.

b. Decide how to use the class time. If individuals prepare reflection papers or are given assignments, these can be shared. Small groups can be formed, or the class can work as a group. Some may wish to write an autobiographical sketch on an event, or moment, in their life.

c. Prepare your prayer for opening the class, and determine your instructions for the next session.

2. *Welcome the class to another meeting.* By this point, the class should be developing a common life. No doubt there will be comments from members about reconvening. Let these develop as expressions of how individuals are thinking and feeling about the material and the group. Acknowledge the struggle, celebrate the progress, and move directly to your prayer.

3. *Introduce the session's purpose and procedure.* Follow the suggestions made at the close of the last session. On the blackboard, outline the types of exercises in the text, and determine how the class will proceed. Block out the time allocated to the exercises. Remember that two video segments may be used in this session (#5 and #6). Proceed with the exercises.

4. At the agreed upon time, *call the group together and view video #5 and/or #6.* Discuss each.

5. *Return to the exercises in the text* or to other applications the class has chosen.

6. *Bring the class to a close by asking for their assessment of their progress.* Do they have a better understanding of the model? Does it help them in self-understanding or in analysis of common experience?

7. *Make the reading and any other assignments for the next and last session.*

Chapter 6: Living in the Promise

Main Objective

To enable us to understand that conversion is a life-long process of living in the presence of God's gift and promise. This process takes the form of (1) exploring the risks involved in the promise; (2) considering the new being offered in Jesus Christ; (3) asking what we are to become in Jesus Christ.

Basic Methods

1. Review previous chapters and discuss chapter 6.

2. Use and discuss video spots #7 and #8: interviews with people living in the promise.

Suggested Plan

1. *Prepare for the class.*

   a. Review the chapter, and give some thought to the relation of turning away from something to turning to the promise. To what extent has becoming something new been a major factor in your life or the life of your congregation? Will the class need some help in understanding why this chapter is included? What does that question say about our understanding of conversion?

   b. Preview video spots #7 and #8. If you will use them in the session, decide when.

   c. Prepare your prayer for the last session. You may also want to prepare a closing prayer of thanksgiving and celebration of the new bonds formed by this class.

2. *Welcome the members to the final session and offer your prayer.*

3. *Determine whether "The Risk of the Promise" speaks to the experience of the class.* Provide opportunity for the class to acknowledge the risk and fear present when we face the issue of change.

4. *Introduce "The New Being in Jesus Christ"* with a key question such as, Do you think anything new in your life is possible? or What is the new reality that makes change possible?

5. As a transition to "Christian Being," you may wish to *use the video spots #7 and #8,* followed by class discussion.

6. *Proceed to "Christian Being."* Form small groups, and let each person answer these questions: What do you expect of God in your life? Have you made any plans for the future in light of your turning to God? What does this congregation expect of God? Does it have any plans for the future?

7. *Bring the session and course to a close.* You may want to ask for comments and reflect on the journey. Some may want to take a next step in pursuing issues raised in the course. Gather up these comments in your closing prayer, and wish the group peace and joy.